D1403402

Marketing by the Numbers

Marketing
by the
Numbers

How to Measure and Improve
the ROI of Any Campaign

**Leland Harden
and Bob Heyman**

ᴀMACOM

American Management Association
New York • Atlanta • Brussels • Chicago • Mexico City • San Francisco
Shanghai • Tokyo • Toronto • Washington, D.C.

Special discounts on bulk quantities of AMACOM books are available to corporations, professional associations, and other organizations. For details, contact Special Sales Department, AMACOM, a division of American Management Association, 1601 Broadway, New York, NY 10019.
Tel.: 212-903-8316. Fax: 212-903-8083.
Web site: www.amacombooks.org

This publication is designed to provide accurate and authoritative information in regard to the subject matter covered. It is sold with the understanding that the publisher is not engaged in rendering legal, accounting, or other professional service. If legal advice or other expert assistance is required, the services of a competent professional person should be sought.

Harden, Leland.
    Marketing by the numbers : how to measure and improve the ROI of any campaign / Leland Harden and Bob Heyman.
      p. cm.
    Includes bibliographical references and index.
    ISBN-13: 978-0-8144-1620-4
    ISBN-10: 0-8144-1620-9
    1. Internet marketing.   2. Internet marketing—Case studies.   I. Heyman, Bob, 1948–   II. Title.
HF5415.1265.H3665   2010
658.8'02—dc22

2010027228

Printing number

10 9 8 7 6 5 4 3 2 1

Contents

Acknowledgments

THE ART AND SCIENCE of measuring the cost-effectiveness of new media has been a moving target these past several years, and a controversial one at that. The authors would like to thank all our colleagues who have provided insight, argument, and a generous discussion from their own special viewpoints, to help us make this book as pertinent as possible to marketers both online and off.

Our special thanks to Geoff Ramsey and Kris Oser of eMarketer, Gian Fulgoni of comScore, Randall Beard at Nielsen, Jim Sterne at Target Marketing, Gary Angel of Semphonic, Marshall Sponder, Mark Rotblat, Pinny Gniwisch, Andreas Ramos, Akin Arikan, Michael Andrew, James Barnes, Paul Kravitz, Katy (KD) Paine, Marni Baker Stein, Josh Chasin, Pat LaPointe, Pat McGraw, and Jodi McDermott. All are leading lights in this field of endeavor, and worth following on any social media platform they choose to share their data and their experience.

Thanks also to our book editorial team: Ellen Kadin, Executive Editor at AMACOM, Senior Development Editor Barry Richardson, Associate Editor Mike Sivilli, and all their skilled staff; our Content Wrangler Mia Amato; Julia Han, our go-to expert for all things graphic, our superb copyeditor Debbie Posner, and our agent, Neil Salkind.

Thanks also to our families, close friends, and colleagues in Sausalito and Abilene to whom we especially dedicate this book.

—Leland Harden and Bob Heyman

Marketing by the Numbers

CHAPTER 1

Introduction

How to Drive Successful Marketing ROI

THIS BOOK may save your marketing life.

We don't have to tell you things are tough out there. It doesn't matter if you are a profitable commerce engine, a nonprofit, an educational institution, or a government entity with a message to impart. Experienced marketers need to learn new tricks to stay competitive.

The techniques and best practices recommended for web marketing aren't just replacing traditional marketing spending, they're *driving* traditional marketing spending. How often do you see a car commercial on television that doesn't include a website URL? Why does every trade magazine you subscribe to have an online version? When you shop at a favorite store, do you bring in downloaded coupons?

As for your own marketing efforts:

▶ How often do you integrate your own online/offline strategies?

▶ Do you measure effective spending across multiple media?

> ▶ Are you familiar with the marketing analytics your CFO looks at most?

If you don't have clear answers to all three of these questions, it's time to sharpen all your marketing strategies, online and off. Most of the tools you will need are free and some are even familiar.

Advances in marketing analytics make accurate return on investment (ROI) more possible than ever before. The metrics of traditional marketing vehicles—direct mail, print, TV, radio, and environmental media—are now being reassessed by marketers and agencies whose clients are asking them to do more with less. Where useful, they will continue to be utilized. But in today's marketing environment, many of the older methods used to measure the value of marketing media have been found to be false, fuzzy, and inaccurate. As marketing budgets get tighter, many of us find there is no room for strategies that do not materially and directly contribute to the health of an enterprise that we, as marketers, are responsible for.

We wrote this book because, after the publication of *Digital Engagement* (AMACOM Books, 2009), we found there was still a hunger among marketers, especially those who use the Internet extensively, for solid measurement techniques. A few books out there do discuss marketing ROI in theoretical terms, focusing on the math and on traditional media. There are many books on web media that will tell you how to count your clicks, but rarely do they provide insight into how to drive successful marketing ROI. The opportunity exists to meld both disciplines—marketing finance and marketing analytics—and we feel the time is now.

And for marketers, the need to be up to speed on both may be urgent.

Understanding the marketing spend from a finance department's point of view requires a different sort of bottom-line thinking than what most creative marketers employ day to day. In this book, we hope to help you discover not only ways to get the best return from your marketing dollars, but also ways to communicate the value of your decisions to others in your organization whose financial decisions ultimately affect your own.

ROI: Risk, Not Roll of the Dice

In traditional accounting, return on investment (ROI) is viewed as a *predictive* formula. It's not just a reflection of the past, but a valuable financial forecasting tool. In fact, when accountants over their beers speak of ROI, this is usually what they mean—a calculated mathematical method to estimate and assess the risk of a proposed expenditure that's supposed to result in profit.

Yet in the context of marketing, and especially Internet marketing, ROI is all too often calculated after the fact. You purchased $120,000 for three months of online banner advertising and got five million click-throughs and 40,000 sign-ups to your e-mail newsletter. So what? How many widgets did you sell during that three-month period? How many in the following quarter? How many sales can be directly attributed to leads from your banner campaign?

Connecting your marketing spending to actual sales and revenue has always been a convoluted path, but never a more urgent one than today. The rise of the web as the most measurable means of tracking marketing spending has had ripples throughout marketing disciplines, from the simple direct-mail response rates of decades ago to the latest methods to track "sentiment" in Facebook and Twitter conversations. Online, the accountability to be found in web metrics makes the process transparent, and it is possible to review the ROI of every single part of your customer outreach, individually and as a whole.

This works even if you are literally selling nuts and bolts. Ace Hardware (see Case Study #1) is one of the 5 percent of companies that sell products online offering not just direct shipping to customers, but an option for "free" shipping to the store that is nearest the customer. At Ace, 80 percent of online orders now ship to stores, with more than 30 percent of customers purchasing an additional item once they arrive in the store. Benefits in the mix include smaller store inventories, the lower costs of customer-initiated online sales, shipping cost savings, incremental revenues, and a perfect fit to the "do-it-yourself" customer of this hardware store chain. The beauty of it is that all of this is trackable—online orders can be matched to cash register data, and good customers can be identified for other marketing outreach.

And, even if your marketing plans include no Internet spending, or it's only a minor line item in your budget, you'll have to pay attention to techniques and trends in online ROI, because the same detailed level of accountability is now being focused on all other forms of traditional marketing media—TV, radio, print, trade shows, catalogs, direct mail, etc.

Traditional Marketing Media

In 2009, the research chiefs of fourteen major media outlets, including ABC, CBS, NBC, CNN, ESPN, Fox, MTV, and their counterparts in the advertising world, formed a new organization, the Council for Innovative Media Measurement, which aimed to look at the older, traditional methods of counting and paying for audiences, and use newer methods to help quantify and justify ad spending through both old and new channels, which include video viewed through computers and mobile phones, and radio segments downloaded to MP3 players. No, they said, it wasn't that they were unhappy with Nielsen Ratings that so plainly showed the attrition of their audience to new media. What was wanted—and what their advertisers were asking for—was justification for million-dollar campaigns that were spread over multiple channels.

Advertisers, meanwhile, are voting with their feet and heading for the exits—or at least into lower priced cable television and web TV. When Pepsi decides to forego its traditional Super Bowl advertising after decades of high-tech visuals and high-priced buys, as it did in 2010, it was hardly surprising to find even Rupert Murdoch predicting the imminent demise of ad-supported broadcast television.

We've since seen some interesting developments in correlating cross-channel branding with sales data. Nielsen's Homescan unit, in cooperation with Yahoo!, tracks online ad exposures among panels of shoppers. In December 2009, Nielsen took another step with Nielsen Catalina Ventures to create the first "TV return on investment measurement service" using data from the same Homescan box, to correlate TV watching behaviors with Internet use and purchase data from an estimated 50 million shoppers who receive print marketing materials through Catalina Marketing's retailer network. And Nielsen has continued to explore new methods to track new kinds of information marketers have asked for, including soft metrics such as "buzz"—an attempt to measure word-of-mouth marketing and product reputation representing excitement and conversation about a product or service—and harder data attempting to match up Internet chatter with TV ad placements.

One might argue that the inability to link print advertising impact with actual sales was a deciding factor in the demise of glossy magazines such as *Gourmet, Architectural Digest,* and *Southern Living,* and trade publications such as *Editor & Publisher* and *Fortune Small Business*. In 2009, Crain's reported 367 North American glossies perished, and a number of major market newspapers—the *Seattle Post-Intelligencer, Rocky Mountain News*—folded, while the *Los Angeles Times* and *Chicago Tribune* drifted into bankruptcy. Tablet computers, which have the ability to track online purchases to links in online publications, may not be the total savior of the newspaper business but a number of glossies—among them *Gourmet*—have since reappeared as an application for the iPad.

And even as magazine ad page sales have rebounded in 2010, such shifts in media platforms are significant and put the traditional marketing manager at risk.

Online Marketing Metrics

It's no longer enough to drop $250,000 annually on your corporate website without requiring, at the end of the year, some concrete indication of how that spending resulted in actual revenue. Under the ROI microscope, the website is no longer overhead—it's a profit center and it needs to be profitable. The $50,000 allotted each year for a local sports team sponsorship is no longer viewed by management as a mere branding exercise. In 2010 and beyond, the sponsorship is more likely to be viewed as a lead-generation vehicle, to be measured against other lead-generating initiatives in the same market, such as ads in a local newspaper.

Is this unfair? Probably. Is this the future? We think so. According to Forrester Research, U.S. companies spent $421 million on web analytics programs that include data analysis of advertising campaign performance, and the research firm predicts that spending will more than double to $953 million by 2014.

Figure 1-1. Ad spending projections 2010.

	2007	2008	2009	2010	2011
Newspapers	27.0	25.3	23.8	22.5	21.6
Magazines	12.1	11.5	10.9	10.4	10.1
Television	37.4	38.1	38.6	39.3	39.2
Radio	8.0	7.8	7.5	7.3	7.2
Cinema	.05	.05	.05	.05	.06
Outdoor	6.4	6.5	6.5	6.6	6.7
Internet	8.7	10.4	12.1	13.3	14.6

Source: Zenith Optimedia

All mass media ad spending will be expected to be as targeted and performance-oriented as web ad spending is. And—should you have spent the last five years marketing under a rock—web ad spending is no longer a small line item in a marketer's budget. According to figures released in November 2009 by PricewaterhouseCoopers and the Interactive Advertising Bureau (IAB), U.S. online ad spending in the third quarter reached $5.5 billion. And this was in a year of decline; the same study reported those dollars were down 5.4 percent from the same period, Q3 in 2007.

In desperation, online marketers are throwing more dollars into search—about 7 percent more in Q4 2009. A good chunk of that went to a new player—Bing, the search engine launched by Microsoft Network (MSN) in the summer of 2009. Bing became the default search engine loaded with Internet Explorer in the newest shipments of personal computers and portable PCs (replacing the Google search field). U.S. retailers responded to Bing by increasing paid search there by 47 percent over what they'd spent the year before on the older MSN. When holiday sales had settled, and were found to be at par or slightly below 2008's rather grim revenues, even this leap of faith seemed to be a mistake in hindsight. So why are search and e-mail still the dominant forms of online marketing? The main reason is because they are measurable. Not because they work like a charm every time.

Marketing Through Social Media

In 2009 we saw growth in marketing dollars spent on online social media—another leap of faith. According to eMarketer, sales of paid social network advertising hit $1.2 billion, and are expected to rise to $1.3 billion during 2010.

If someone in your organization (or you) are planning to explore social media such as Facebook and Twitter as a medium for ad messages, a January 2010 study by MarketingProfs of about 5,000 business-to-business (B-to-B) and business-to-consumer (B-to-C) web marketers may be of interest. (The entire 242-page report, *The State of Social Media*, may be accessed at www.marketingprofs.com.) The study found that the tactics used most often to drive traffic to company websites were not the most successful. The results reflect what we already know from several years of social media exploration.

For example, it's not surprising that constant status updates, like multiple e-mails, fail to deliver anything but customer fatigue. Attempts to drive traffic with Twitter posts were the most common strategy, and the least effective. Why? Because it's a mass-market, scattershot technique that's not applicable to the conversational nature of social media. (We'd call it a direct descendant of the telemarketing call found on your voicemail or answering machine.) What did work on Twitter was engaging customers directly: inviting Twitter users to special in-person events worked for both business audiences and consumers.

On Facebook, what worked was engaging readers by soliciting

them to "friend" a company page or by eliciting commentary through a survey (see Figure 1-2). Buying ads on social media sites—even "targeted" ads—were the least effective, a real waste of dollars.

The Facebook statistics may be useful for all networking sites, such as LinkedIn for professionals (www.linkedin.com). For example, creating an application (app) for Facebook users to share worked for consumer marketers, and a consumer products company might comfortably investigate creating free apps for smartphones.

More than half of the respondents in the study also reported monitoring Twitter for PR problems (see Figure 1-3). And probably many of them use the fee-based "listening" services to track negative or positive brand comments, as determined by sentiment analysis. But in this survey, only 22 percent of monitoring companies took the logical additional step of contacting social media users who posted negative comments.

Overall, it's easy to see that marketers are falling into the same trap as the respondents in the MarketingProfs survey: spending on cheaper, automated solutions, rather than using social media to reach out and communicate with their audiences. This has implications not just for marketing, but for public relations as well.

Marketing's more glamorous sister—public relations—is even

Figure 1-2. Facebook tactics.

Successful Facebook Marketing Tactics used by B2B and B2C (n = 643 marketers)	B2B	B2C
Created a survey of "fans"	37.1%	37.9%
"Friending" recent customers with corporate Facebook profile	34.4%	26.3%
Used Facebook user data to profile customers or interests	33.5%	30.5%
Created a Facebook application around a brand	33.1%	30.5%
Driving traffic to corporate materials with status updates	29.0%	28.4%
Buying targeted CPC ads of Facebook	24.5%	27.1%

Source: MarketingProfs, "The State of Social Media," December 2009, via eMarketer

Figure 1-3. Twitter strategies.

Successful Twitter Marketing Tactics used by B2B and B2C (n = 722 B2B, 329 B2C marketers using Twitter)	B2B	B2C
Monitor Twitter for PR problems in real time	40.7%	46.9%
Created in-person event using only Twitter invites	37.5%	36.0%
Driving traffic by linking to marketing webpages	36.7%	44.0%
Provocative text to drive clicks	35.7%	35.2%
Cultivate Twitter users with positive brand tweets	34.8%	40.6%
Increased "followers" by traditional media mentions	34.0%	33.9%
Timing tweets to maximize views	30.7%	30.4%
Driving sales by linking to promotional webpages	22.4%	24.6%

Source: MarketingProfs, "The State of Social Media," December 2009, via eMarketer

more at risk and under fire in the new world of measurable web media. In hard economic times, PR is always the first on the chopping block. There's no excuse today to rely on "soft" data when product excitement, or buzz, is now being quantified in scary ways. There are new data to be harvested—it's called "engagement" or "sentiment analysis." Like older forms of word-of-mouth marketing, word-of-web or viral media is recognized as a powerful marketing tool. What's not clear is how to measure its impact in either direct sales or brand awareness. Yet for this, a whole crop of computerized tools and specialty outsource companies that did not exist three years ago are knocking at the door, and it would be a mistake not to recognize who they are, what they can do, and which you'll need to survive.

New tools to develop brand awareness in the online space should be in every marketing manager's portfolio, whether or not you are also responsible for public relations, investor relations, or customer service.

For example: even if the company views its website as a purely promotional or branding expense, activities surrounding it are called into question every day. If a single blog mention brings 370,000 first-time visitors to a brand website, how do you justify the cost of producing a television spot—with URL included—that brought in fewer than 500,000 first-timers? Now it's too, too easy to prove that your clever celebrity video on YouTube was a real bust, because the number of times a clip was viewed is a number just below the clip—a number that's visible to anyone, including the CEO's grandniece.

For nonprofits, the need to explore social media without overspending staff time or other resources is going to continue unabated. Of 200 nonprofit executives polled recently by KRC Research (part of the agency Interpublic), 88 percent experimented with social media at least once in 2009, and 85 percent planned to use it again in 2010. Do

Figure 1-4. This video had been seen by 120,889 viewers at the time of this screen grab.

the math and you get seventeen executives who either got burned or found their expectations did not measure up in ROI.

At present there are more than 100 service companies eager to provide your organization with "listening" services that will monitor tweets and news and blog postings to tell you whether you're loved or hated online. It is far better to be proactive, as Veolia Water, a French company selected to operate a new wastewater treatment plant in the Marin County suburb of Novato, learned the hard way. When a local newspaper revealed that Veolia had donated $25,000 to the 2009 election campaigns of incumbents who served as directors for the water utility, irate bloggers spread the story nationally. For weeks, any attempt to call up the company's website in search was topped off with negative comments from blogs. A significant investment in paid search was required to get the corporate websites top billing (literally). This was unfortunate, as the company had a similar operation in Indianapolis, with a sunny, consumer-friendly website well in place. Had Veolia made a new local website earlier, curious local customers and news organizations would have found a source for the company's take on the news. Today, Veolia has a continuing presence on LinkedIn, Twitter, and recently began outreach on Facebook. They learned the hard way. You don't have to.

Where's Your Audience?

You can talk all you want about targeted marketing, but if your target has shifted the media it attends to, you and your analytics must follow.

Some thought a dip in the U.S. economy might spur more TV watching, if folks stayed home to save their entertainment dollars. Incoming Nielsen reports, which tend to be TV-friendly, are corroborating independent surveys that show at least a third of all television viewing is done over Internet channels, such as YouTube, Hulu.com, Veoh.com, and the websites of TV and cable networks. They're also renting movies on DVD, from the ubiquitous NetFlix or from their local public library: libraries in major cities such as New York, Los Angles, Cleveland, and San Jose allow their patrons to download movies directly into their computers for viewing at home.

Younger consumers also attend to their mobile telephones for more than just chats. Web-enabled mobile phones allow them to enter contests by texting, search for local restaurants and specialty stores through geocentric ad placements, and network socially with their friends. All ages equipped with web-ready phones now get the latest sports news and weather, plus music, *without ever once turning on a radio.*

The rise of the Internet as a communications and sales medium over the past ten years has been a juggernaut, if you believe the results of a Pew Research Center study on Internet Life released in November 2009. In the year 2000, 46 percent of U.S. adults used the web; by 2009, the percentage was 79 percent. By 2009, 63 percent of households had broadband, meaning home computers could access streaming video, animations, and music, compared to 5 percent in 2000. By 2009 approximately 55 percent of U.S. adults had access to a wireless Internet connection, through devices such as web-enabled phones, netbooks, and PDAs not yet invented ten years earlier.

Search, shopping, e-mail, and peer exchange are in use by all demographics; according to web research group comScore and Facebook itself, the fastest growing demographic for the social networking site (www.facebook.com) for the past two years has been women aged 55 and up. ComScore reports the age range for Twitter is between 25 and 55. Tracking a single month in August 2009, Nielsen found that 17 percent of time spent online by its panelists was spent at social networking sites, compared to 6 percent the year before.

The Pew study also found 9 percent of Americans were likely to visit an online classified ad site, such as Craigslist.org. And everybody shopped, with the lion's share of purchasing going to well-branded sites such as Amazon.com.

On the web, an estimated 30 percent of visits to U.S.-based websites come from abroad. That's great if you're selling a global product that can be squeezed through an Internet connection: distance learning, software, digital entertainment products, or ideas and concepts to better humanity.

For everyone else, the home page needs a protocol to channel those visitors to overseas affiliates. It's usually a link or series of links. Federal Express, Apple Computer, and the individual product lines of Procter & Gamble (see www.pampers.com) do an excellent job of redirecting traffic so no sales are lost.

Domestically, adding Spanish, Mandarin, or Korean language pages is a trend worth following. The global networking site Facebook allows user setting to more than fifty languages, including some made-up ones (Esperanto and Pirate; see Figure 1-5). This has allowed them to become the dominant social networking site not just in North America, but in Mexico, Germany, and India so far.

We'd suggest that all organizations selling domestically look at multicultural opportunities to gain new customers. Some of the "research" in this area, though, practically borders on the stereotypical—Hispanics spend more on babies and children, African Americans watch more TV and have more mobile phones, Asians are more likely to eat at restaurants, etc. For your own product, and for your own market, you should always test both the message and the channel. Fortunately, there are many, many new channels to experiment with—ethnic radio, cable TV, and of course foreign language publications and social media networks.

The other area to look at in depth is mobile advertising, which

Figure 1-5. Facebook's "Pirate" setting.

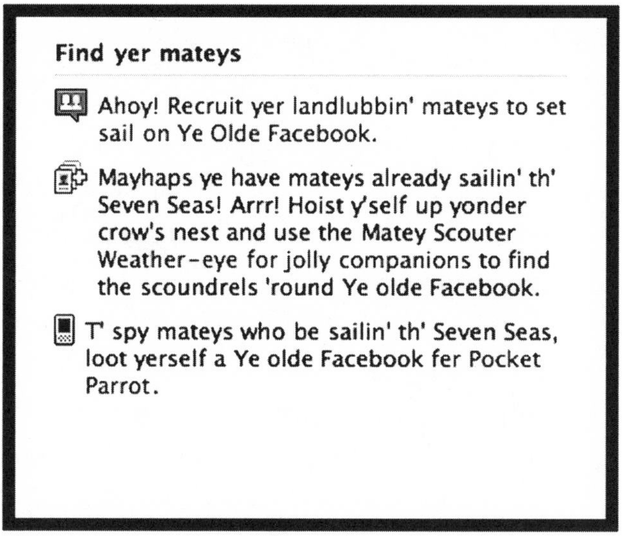

Find yer mateys

Ahoy! Recruit yer landlubbin' mateys to set sail on Ye Olde Facebook.

Mayhaps ye have mateys already sailin' th' Seven Seas! Arrr! Hoist y'self up yonder crow's nest and use the Matey Scouter Weather-eye for jolly companions to find the scoundrels 'round Ye olde Facebook.

T' spy mateys who be sailin' th' Seven Seas, loot yerself a Ye olde Facebook fer Pocket Parrot.

embraces many languages yet has the capability to geoposition your marketing message to an individual who may be standing on a street corner searching for your product or service. By February 2010 the largest global market share of portable phones was being led by iPhone and Android OS devices, which include web browsing and GPS features.

In other words, modern marketing isn't just about finding your customer. More and more it's about newer strategies that allow the customer to find *you*, within a window of time that facilitates a near-immediate (and yes trackable) purchase. This is way beyond sending out a branding message and hoping for "recall" during a shopping trip.

Traditional Media in Transition

So, what's a ROI target for marketing investments these days? According to The Nielsen Company, long a bellwether for marketing statistics, the average return for a marketing spend globally is about 9 percent for a three-month campaign.

These figures come from a published report that focused largely on Asian markets, a growth area for both consumer and business products and services. Based on a number of studies worldwide, the report analyzed both traditional and new media, and found (interestingly enough) that online advertising had a better return ($2.18 for the dollar) than magazine ads ($1.12 per dollar) and newspapers were found to be underperforming, with only 24 cents of incremental revenue accrued for every dollar spent. See Figure 1-6.

We find much to quibble with on this chart and its attendant report. For starters, the survey disproportionally examines Asian marketing spends, which may not apply to media vehicles in the United

Figure 1-6. ROI benchmarks in worldwide media.

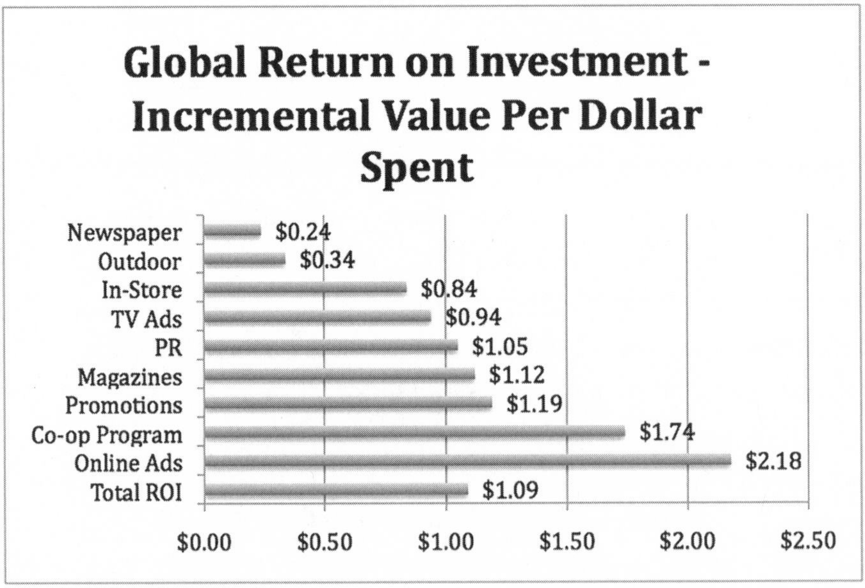

Global Return on Investment - Incremental Value Per Dollar Spent

Media	Value
Newspaper	$0.24
Outdoor	$0.34
In-Store	$0.84
TV Ads	$0.94
PR	$1.05
Magazines	$1.12
Promotions	$1.19
Co-op Program	$1.74
Online Ads	$2.18
Total ROI	$1.09

Source: The Nielsen Company

States. We also find it interesting that long-term ROI (over six months) was only measured in television advertising, magazines, and publicity spending. Long-term effects of other brand messages, particularly online display ads and long-running web initiatives, can also be counted if you've got your figures available (see Chapter 2).

Still, a 9 percent benchmark is a good start if you have none of your own, and you can probably do better. One conclusion we heartily agree with is that most companies can increase their ad spending ROI by 40 percent by using multiple channels to bolster a single brand message, and by using your strongest brand to pull along new products (Nielsen calls this the "halo effect"). Note: The full report is available as a downloadable PDF from Nielsen's marketing blog: http://blog.-nielsen.com/nielsenwire/reports/marketing-roi.pdf.

Nielsen is also bullish on TV advertising, not surprising since it began its career as a television ratings company. But marketers are not, or at least were not in 2009, when TV ad spending dropped precipitously in the first three quarters, according to Nielsen's own research.

Buying Media in Recessionary Times

The normal response for marketers in a recession is to cut spending, and that's what happened in 2008 and 2009. Looking at 2010 reporting, U.S. ad spending for traditional media buys dropped between 8 percent and 9 percent in 2009. This followed a drop of about 5 percent in 2008 after some years of modest increases in most sectors.

According to a free report by Nielsen (Figure 1-7), advertisers pulled out of national, regional, and local magazines in droves in 2009, and B-to-B companies bought 30 percent less advertising in business and trade publications last year. Other big media losers were Sunday ad circulars (down 44 percent), and spot TV buys (down approximately 15 percent across the country). Nationally, spending was cut in the automotive sector and in the financial services group. As both of these sectors were involved in controversial government bailout programs, the lower profile is hardly surprising. Overall, spending was down 15 percent through the first six months of 2009, and 11 percent in the holiday-heavy fourth quarter, compared to 2008.

Yet by the last quarter, advertisers did creep back, according to the Nielsen report. National newspapers, which lost more than 20 percent of their revenues in the first three quarters of 2009, picked up a little in the fourth quarter when they cut rates. Magazines that survived the death of their competitors in the last few years saw a slight rise (less than 1 percent on average) in ad page sales in 2010. Television advertisers fled to lower priced cable television, increasing spending in that medium by 14 percent. Freestanding coupon inserts replaced newspaper advertising—and it's worth noting that spending on this far more trackable medium increased more than 10 percent in 2009.

But that wasn't all the news, and the trends are worth looking at.

Ethnic media spending—generally a bargain in terms of cost—actually grew significantly during the latter part of 2009, with Spanish-language cable TV enjoying a 32 percent increase in ad sales nationally. That figure is corroborated by Nielsen and several other industry surveys of 2009, which also report that ad spending on radio advertising targeted to African American audiences increased by 35 percent.

And, of course, Internet display advertising, a decade ago the laughingstock of media buys, grew 32 percent in 2009 according to Nielsen. Not counting paid search but merely graphic and video ads placed online, Internet display accounted for more than a billion dollars in ad sales, even though click-through rates remain abysmal and are expected to remain in the 0.0001 range for the new future. By the way, Nielsen reported that overall Internet spending was "flat"— indicating that as some advertisers pulled out, new advertisers moved

Figure 1-7. Changes in how advertising money was spent, 2008–2009

Media Category	% Change, Jan.–Dec. 2008 Jan.–Dec. 2009
Spanish-Language Cable TV	32.2%
Cable TV	14.8%
FSI Coupon	11.5%
Internet	.01%
Spanish-Language Network TV	− 3.9%
National Sunday Supplement	− 7.2%
Spot Radio	− 8.7%
Network Radio	− 9.7%
Network TV	− 9.9%
Local Newspaper	− 13.7%
Outdoor	− 11.2%
Spot TV 101–210 Markets	− 14.2%
Syndicated TV	− 14.7%
Spot TV Top 100 Markets	− 16.1%
National Magazine	− 19.3%
Local Magazine	− 23.9%
B2B	− 32.7%
Local Sunday Supplment	− 44.9%
Total Average	**− 9.0%**

Source: The Nielsen Company.

in. As a consequence, costs of online advertising have remained fairly constant, even as print and TV costs fell.

GENERALLY SPEAKING, AD SPENDING IS STILL A GOOD INVESTMENT

Bucking the tide, food products marketer General Mills spent 19 percent more on its television advertising in 2009 than it did the year before, and saw its profits climb 49 percent by year's end. In a bad economy, the company bet that consumers would be eating breakfast at home, rather than picking up pricey lattes on the way to office jobs that no longer existed. Accordingly, it ramped up television advertising for traditional cereal brands such as Cheerios, and home biscuit products such as Pillsbury—especially pushing those homemade cinnamon buns that smell just like the ones that perfume your local mall. Another effort was made with a betty-crocker.com website, which required registration but offered "more than one hundred dollars" of coupons for the company's nationally recognized brands.

Halfway through its fiscal year, General Mills was sufficiently pleased with its efforts to present the results at a conference of the Consumer Analysts Group of New York. Ian Friendly, COO of U.S. retail operations, said the company looked at emerging markets beyond the traditional grocery store customer. Drugstores, dollar-store discounters, and Hispanic markets were new targets for distribution. For advertising, the new targets were Hispanic consumers, a growing segment of the U.S. population, and baby boomers, which Friendly noted accounts for half of the U.S. population in 2010.

Friendly credited Hispanic-targeted television advertising with a 35 percent increase in sales for Honey Nut Cheerios, after noting that the company had increased Hispanic-targeted media spending by 70 percent for that product. Bromley Communications, based in San Antonio, would later win industry awards (including the 2009 ARF Gold Ogilvy Award) for the Honey Nuts Cheerios campaign, which has expanded to include Internet display advertising.

For baby boomers, Cheerios commercials, advertisements, and even product boxes touted the benefits of oat cereal—such as lowering cholesterol and preventing heart disease. Some of these health claims actually got the company stern scrutiny from the FDA, though while some box language has been altered, the halo effect stayed with the product

General Mills also dipped into the social media stream to promote its Yoplait yogurt line among boomer's children, defined as those aged 16 to 33. A sexy commercial showing attractive women blissfully spooning up a "satisfying" snack aired in both English and Spanish, got ogled, passed around, and commented on YouTube. Bloggers and web influentials in the parenting community (mommy bloggers) were courted with samples, coupons, and prize packs to promote Yoplait Kids, resulting in 300,000 coupon downloads from the main website. As for the bettycrocker.com site, it typically receives about 8 million visits per month. While that number may vary, its downloadable coupon program allows for tracking and testing against retail sales.

General Mills executives such as Mark Addicks, chief marketing officer, point out that social media is a natural extension of how household product brands are best promoted: through word of mouth. Legacy products typically have fan communities; the challenge is promoting older products to new customers. It's also important to note that ad spending by itself was not the only strategy to find these new customers: new package designs and entirely new products (such as a canned menudo meal from the Progresso brand line) were also tested.

Again: Where's Your Audience?

Television, radio, newspapers, magazines, and direct mail aren't going to go away. You're just going to be buying these media in a slightly different way. This means you will spend more on more targeted media, to seek new customers to balance off the lower revenues you may be seeing from your existing customers.

Let's take a look at television, for example. General Mills (see box), purveyor of legacy brands for breakfast cereals, has never had a strong web presence and probably hasn't really needed one to get you to buy a box of Cheerios. But it did have a real problem back in 2008— profits were down and it missed its earnings expectations on Wall Street, one of several major brands to feel the impact of the economic slump during this period.

As described above, General Mills took a bold step in 2009: it raised its advertising spending 19 percent in the first half of the year, while its main competitors, Kellogg's and Kraft Foods, scaled back. When sales increased by at least 10 percent for the period, it launched a fall television offensive, with an emphasis on targeting new audiences by moving dollars into Spanish-language media as well as moving media buys from children's programming to TV shows that attracted baby boomers. Television commercials showed adults, not just children, eating cereals, while younger viewers were wooed with social media coupon campaigns for General Mills's Yoplait yogurt line.

The results were impressive: General Mills overall saw a 5 percent increase in retail net sales in the United States for 2009. It ended the year with earnings up, stock up, and a market-proven strategy for bringing new customers to its legacy brands.

Kantar Media, part of the WPP agency group, surveyed major U.S. advertisers and found that while some advertisers pulled back drastically in 2009, others increased their ad spending in traditional media. Procter & Gamble, the top advertiser in America and a fairly healthy corporate entity, cut spending in 2009 by 15 percent overall. General Motors, which suffered not only a bad-press bailout but also an actual bankruptcy, stayed the course on its media spending and actually increased its budget by 1 percent. Other big spenders were Pfizer, upping the ante for Viagra, and Wal-Mart, seeking new budget-conscious consumers, both increasing ad spends by more than 30 percent in 2009. In the telecommunications space, Sprint Nextel increased its ad budget 29 percent and poured a lot of that into non-English-language media.

These days Nielsen and its nearest rivals—including the promising technology from TRA (www.traglobal.com) and a 2010 iPhone initiative from the Council for Innovative Media Measurement—are busily integrating web, mobile phone, and traditional television into what is often called a "three-screen" approach to recapture the old television audience of yore. Their research suggests that 15 million Americans watch at least three hours of television per month on their mobile phones. As for regular television viewing, nearly 60 percent of TV viewers use the web at the same time. Simultaneous viewing while tweeting or texting, and viewing while talking on a cell phone, is pretty common among younger consumers who can simultaneously plan their weekend while shopping for the outfit they just saw on *Gossip Girl*. The trend isn't restricted to kids, as older adults and families watch awards telecasts "together" via phone, or banter with other sports fans during televised games.

To make this easier, Comcast and other cable/Internet providers, as well as television set manufacturers, now offer televisions that have Internet screens. The Macintosh iPad, built for Internet access as well as for viewing of live-streaming video, takes the TV/web combo down to the size and portability of a newsstand magazine.

What Are You Really Measuring?

General Mills has got a lot right—including the fact that it measures its success in marketing by how much revenue the company's various units bring in. Those marketers who swapped out print ads for locally mailed or inserted coupons could also test and measure the ROI of their spending.

Yet for many TV advertisers, the flimflam of soft metrics can obscure the issue of profitability. One troubling trend we've seen is efforts by advertising agencies and media sites to force the old broken system of GRPs (gross rating points) onto the newer disciplines of cross-channel marketing. This is a big mistake. But it's easy to see why they're doing it. Ad agencies have made millions and grown their global enterprises by convincing marketers that soft metrics such as "impressions," "reach," and "frequency" are indicators of success. Simply shoehorning them into some kind of numerical system does not make them any more reliable measurements for ROI.

Let's take a look at a recent experiment by Nielsen during the

Super Bowl XLIV telecast of 2010. The test was for a new metric dubbed "BMS" (for Blended Media Score), which looked at factors in both "paid media" and "earned media" during the telecast.

In the study, "paid media" factors included results of ad recall polling, total paid sponsorship (commercial time), and estimated viewership during the telecast as defined by traditional measures of audience and reach figures. The "earned media" factors looked at things like "brand buzz"—basically, the researchers looked at volume of twittering, sentiment analysis of same, and/or whether the total of Facebook followers increased during or after the telecast. With an estimated 105 million viewers tuning in to the game on a variety of screens, and a likely 60 percent of them also texting, updating their Facebook status, or twittering their own commentary at the same time, this looked like a worthwhile experiment to try.

Guess what? When all the factors were weighted, measured in, and compared, Budweiser managed to get the highest BMS score during the 2010 Super Bowl (242 points) while the next highest was Doritos (225 points). So, the brands that fared best during a televised football game were for *beer and chips*. Hardly astounding news, and perhaps a useful validation of the proposed BMS metric. But while we applaud everyone for their serious work in trying to define the impact of social media buzz, the best measurement of branding success is still revenue, and that's what your ROI should reflect.

The Challenge Ahead

Here are a few problems you may have on the road to learning to drive successful marketing ROI:

1. Finding ways to measure ROI across all marketing initiatives (see the University of Pennsylvania's ROI grid, Figure 2-1 in Chapter 2).
2. Dealing with too much data: how to find relevance in a sea of fuzzy web metrics (see "Don't Drown in Data" in Chapter 2).
3. Aligning measurables to ROI (see "Classic ROI Formulas" in Chapter 2).
4. Evaluating quantitative measurements of your marketing spend (see Chapter 3).
5. Evaluating qualitative factors, including social media (see Chapter 3).
6. Understanding the latest analytics tools to apply to ROI (see Chapter 6).
7. Communicating ROI results to the C-suite and building a ROI culture within your marketing department or into the entire enterprise (see Chapter 7).

We feel this last is a group of important skills for any marketing manager. It's not enough to devise clever web dashboards for your own use, and it's poor business to let the IT department, sales department, customer services group, or human resources control what data you have access to. If you cannot achieve transparency to get the data you need to calculate the benefits of the marketing dollars you spend, then at least you need to know how to encourage your own marketing team to understand the spending you are responsible for.

Not only have marketing dollars become scarcer, it has become increasingly more difficult to justify any spending when sales results can be viewed by a C-level executive on a daily basis. This accountability is a trend not likely to subside in this decade.

The pressure comes from even higher up the ladder: according to

Bob Liodice, president of the Association of National Advertisers, "Marketers have been challenged to be more accountable by CEOs who are looking for shareholder return and value. . . . The challenge for marketing is: Prove to me that marketing works. Prove to me that no matter how you slice it, the investments are paying back in both short- and long-term deliverables."

An interesting survey done in 2009 by JupiterResearch and the Verse Group found that "achieving measurable ROI on marketing efforts" was the number-one priority for the marketers polled. Second on the priority list: developing marketing programs that integrate and allow the comparison of offline and traditional media.

The best defense for a marketing manager is to get ROI religion. It's time to dust off and reclaim the financial analytical tools from the accounting silo, add web-based ROI analytics to the mix, and thrive.

CASE STUDY #1

Ace Hardware: Supporting Brick and Mortar with Online Ordering

Ace Hardware is an independently owned and operated chain of stores specializing in hardware and home improvement products, with 2008 online sales of $11.8 million. While this makes it one of the 500 top retail websites in the United States, what's strikingly different about Ace is how its online sales operation pushes traffic to its brick-and-mortar stores. Mark Lowe, eCommerce Marketing Supervisor for Ace, credits one specific strategy, known as Ace Hardware's "ship-to-store" program, which is popular with customers and store owners too.

While ship-to-store is not new (Barnesandnoble.com pioneered this back in the 1990s), the Ace experience is one that even a single-store enterprise might try.

As Lowe explains, there are two channels for purchasing: local stores and dealers (about 4,600) and AceHardware.com. On the website, customers are given the option to either ship to their home or ship to their local Ace. When a customer selects ship-to-store service, orders are fulfilled out of the warehouse for shipping to the local Ace—at no charge to the customer. The delivery is combined with normal deliveries of stock to the stores, which typically "receive one or two trucks per week," notes Lowe. "We have fourteen different retail support centers across the country that we leverage to support our ship-to-store program. When the consumer orders an item, we put it on the very next truck going to that store."

Delivery time range is from one day to about one week. The website also offers UPS options for ship to home. "Those vary, between three to five days for shipping depending on where the customer lives and what they ordered," declares Lowe. "But really, the value of ship-to-store comes into play with what we're selling online. Consumers are buying some really large items, like patio furniture and grills. So the savings to them is significant to ship it to Ace for free versus by UPS to their home, which can get rather expensive. That savings value most of the time outweighs any delay that they would receive in shipment."

That value proposition encourages the customer to use free shipping to their local Ace, especially since the website does not offer free-shipping promotions typical of other online retailers. Results: about 73 percent of Acehard ware.com orders are going ship to store, accounting for 80 percent of the website's online order revenues and the majority of its sales volume.

The ship-to-store option is not only popular with customers, it's a big hit with storeowners too. Says Lowe, "We know that 33 percent of our customers, when they go in the store to pick up their item, purchase an additional item in-store. So we see about a third of those customers buying something else. That's a great value for our stores."

Ace began the ship-to-store program in 2003, and since the number of customers and their order values are captured online and in store receipts, Ace has got a pretty big handle on ROI for the strategy. Items that have been ordered online are charged when the item leaves the warehouse: "We don't want to have merchandise out there that hasn't been paid for," explains Lowe. "We don't want to burden our stores with having to take that credit card transaction." But still, he notes, "We also get good feedback from our stores. They really enjoy the fact that, even though the transaction occurred online, we're giving them the opportunity to see that customer and win that customer over, and show them everything that their store has to offer when the customer actually does come in and pick it up."

Lowe was also kind enough to share some demographic data. Age and income levels are similar to website and in-store shoppers, but the type of product purchased is often quite different. For one thing, the average online ticket is about four times higher than the average in-store ticket.

"I think we were a little surprised early on by how consumers were gravitating to some of the larger ticket items on our site," he notes. These include expensive power tools, industrial-grade equipment such as power washers, and manly toys such as gas-powered outdoor barbecue grills. For these items, customers typically comparison-shop, and online they can view a fuller selection of items than might be available at any one store. They're also big and heavy, so cost of direct shipping to home would likely be a barrier to purchase. This is where the option really shines.

"For example, if their faucet breaks, they're going to have to go into their local Ace to get that repaired today. But if they're looking for a grill, they may be doing some comparison shopping, and they want to see our full selection. We see those orders transacting online. So that kind of plays into our strategy of ship-to-store, because that's where consumers are saving the money, for shipping of those large items."

The system is not without its glitches. For example, it's impossible for a customer to check online to see whether a local Ace Hardware has the item in stock, and that's a feature offered by competing hardware retailers such as Home Depot. Says Lowe, "We're a dealer-owned cooperative, so all of our stores are independently owned and operated. Not all of them are on the same point-of-sale system, so we don't have access to real-time inventory for all of our stores. It's something that we'd eventually like to get." And, due to shipping expenses, while customers in the continental United States pay no shipping fee for ship-to-store, there are small charges for customers who request shipping to stores based in Alaska and Hawaii.

Getting a buy-in from storeowners is critical. Lowe said the expectation for the ship-to-store strategy was that perhaps 50 percent of customers would choose the option, instead of the current 75 percent. This has certainly helped, but in day-day-to-day operations this means ensuring that stores are aware of the orders coming in, and how to contact customers who have an order waiting more than a day or two in the back room. Training is also an issue: employees need to know how to handle an online order that has already been paid for, how to ring up the extra items the customer has picked up during the store visit, and how to handle returns for online purchases. Customers also need to be contacted (usually by e-mail) when the order has been delivered, with information included about where and how to pick up their orders when they arrive at the store.

Says Lowe, "My advice to retailers would be to make it as easy as possible for their stores to execute on their end. Retailers have a lot going on in their stores every day, and this is just an additional responsibility that you're asking them to handle. So making it as easy as possible for them to receive those orders, give it to the customer during pickup, and then, if necessary, take that return. I think it's really important that if you allow ship to store, you also allow them to return the product in-store."

He adds, "We really had no idea how successful it would end up being. If you would have told me back in 2003 that we would send three-quarters of our orders to stores, that would have been hard for me to believe. We thought we were going to see a little bit more of a 50/50 split. But we knew that there was a market for people who wanted to save on shipping. We have 4,600 stores across the country. It was just kind of a no-brainer at that time, and it's definitely exceeded our expectations."

The bottom line: "Making it enticing for them to select that offer for ship to store. In our case, it's the free shipping and then the convenience of the number of locations that we have."

CHAPTER 2

Principles for Measuring Marketing ROI

What to Measure and How to Measure It

COMPUTERS HAVE MADE practically everything easily measurable. Yet, their ubiquity is quite likely to make a marketing manager quite miserable. Why? Because the C-suite knows that every dollar spent on what is now routine online marketing can typically be counted back very specifically, to fractions of a penny, to sales results. This is especially true if you're talking about marketing expenses and the marketing ROI derived from paid search, pay-per-click web banner campaigns, web affiliate programs, or the response rate of an e-mail campaign.

Today, this kind of trackable performance is increasingly being requested for other kinds of marketing expenses, including awareness campaigns, sampling programs, print advertising, even billboards. If your organization is currently pursuing newer forms of online outreach, such as social media or gaming, the push is on to link the costs of these programs to revenues as well.

How can this be done?

This chapter will help you determine how to calculate marketing ROI for every campaign tactic you are using. You'll learn how to prioritize your own key metrics, particularly for new media—how to effectively measure them, monitor them, and communicate them to the rest of the organization so they will have some value—in other words, so they may result in actionable items that will move your business forward.

Defining Marketing ROI

Classic marketing ROI uses common terms and phrases from the finance sector and we'll use them here. Other terms used in marketing may come up, but if you're looking for real ROI data, sticking to the basics is indeed best practice.

Let's be very clear here about what is *not* marketing ROI: counting "impressions" for cost per thousand (CPM) purchases of ad media; measuring brand awareness with surveys; or being able to say that you distributed 20,000 key chains with your company logo on it at a recently sponsored sporting event.

Such branding initiatives are soft data that may or may not result in desirable outcomes—such as actual sales, or sales leads derived from sign-ups to a subscription for a company newsletter or e-mail list. True, these are often paid for out of the marketing budget, but it is important to separate them out—and place them where they belong in your ROI equations. Otherwise you will drown in soft data, and it will be even harder to measure the effectiveness of dollars spent on this campaign versus that one.

There are some practices from new media we can borrow to help you identify and track even soft data. Actual sales and sales leads and other desirable outcomes and audience actions can all fall under the term of *conversions*. Conversions are *results*, and even if the results yield only soft data, these can be tracked and counted against your marketing efforts.

But not all conversions are pertinent, and only a few are real ROI.

This is also *not* marketing ROI: the resulting statistics sent back from your Google Adwords; click-through response rates (CTRs) from your paid search or banner ad programs; the amount of traffic to your website on any given day, relative to your current Facebook campaign, Twitter initiative, blog mention, or e-mail blast.

The numbers crunched from online marketing reports are useful, but at best, they only reflect the discipline of *web analytics*. Web analytics isn't ROI. It's a tool to help you develop the ROI reporting that all companies need for strategic marketing, budget planning, and—the main concern here—a more efficient distribution of marketing dollars and resources within the enterprise.

The range of Google products makes a good example—Adwords, AdSense, and the newer ad platforms available through their purchase of DoubleClick and mobile distributor AdMob. The free web analytics tools that come with these products often give novice marketers the illusion that they're producing reports that reflect actual return on investment. But while they do reflect dollars paid out, they can only "return" statistics to help justify the investment when you look at them through traditional ROI formulas.

Formulas for ROI Measurement

Formulas useful for marketing research, budget planning, and campaign review fall roughly into three categories: operational formulas, overhead calculation, and performance formulas.

> *Operational formulas:* These are the basic formulas for statistical indictors, such as factory/employee output, basic sales data (adjusted for returns, discounts, inventory turnover, etc.), as well as for factors that represent the relative health and status of the marketing department, or the enterprise as a whole. This includes formulas for liquidity (current cash available to spend), working capital management, receivables management, break-even formulas, and return on assets. You'll find a few of the more helpful ones at the end of this chapter.
>
> *Overhead calculation formulas:* These govern the calculation of overhead expenses that may or may not be charged back to the marketing department. In larger organizations, the marketing department is often presented with a number or a figure to include among expenses, which may or may not be a true reflection of marketing's overhead costs. Allocating the expense of overhead within a marketing department allows for some flexibility, so you should know how to do this effectively. We discuss this in detail at the end of the chapter.
>
> *Performance formulas:* These are ratios and tools to measure perform-

ance, profit and loss, and actual figures that indicate revenue return on investments or other cash outlays. Return on investment is a standardized mathematical formula used in accounting that can be applied to marketing investments in the same way that ROI is calculated for the building of new factories, acquisition or shedding of business units, and hiring of staff.

Your Star Performer: ROI

Yes, ROI is a performance measurement, but not all performance measurements are designed to yield ROI. Soft metrics common to advertising, such as brand awareness, engagement, loyalty, purchase intent, and even "impressions" can help to explain what your money was supposed to do, but they have no place in marketing ROI. In accounting terms, such data are merely termed *proxy measures*.

Here's the formula for classic ROI:

$$\text{(Net Revenues} - \text{Marketing Investment)} \div$$
$$\text{Marketing Investment} \times 100 = \text{ROI\%}$$

In simple English, you derive ROI in three steps using only two numbers:

First, you obtain a dollar figure that represents your *net revenues*, after subtracting a dollar figure that represents your spending, that is, your *marketing investment*.

Second, you take that total (*net revenues* minus *marketing investment*) and divide it by the *marketing investment*.

Third, this number is then multiplied by 100 to achieve the percentage of ROI.

ROI is always expressed as a percentage, as it is meant to be compared to other forms of investment by the organization, or payments that achieve a similar valuable return. This can be the investment in the building of a factory, or it can be socking away several hundred thousand dollars in an interest-bearing bank account. (For a more in-depth explanation of ROI calculations, please see the Special Section at the end of Chapter 7, "ROI Basics.")

It's impossible to estimate the ROI of a marketing initiative unless you have both numbers. *Marketing investment* is usually the one you can get easily, and you start with something you can control: the amount you've budgeted for the project. Typically the cost of the project as a complete marketing investment for the ROI calculation includes a variety of other costs and may include overhead charged to your department or to the specific project.

The other key number in the equation is *net revenues*; this number represents the profit (or loss) resulting from the initiative for the period of time being examined.

Basic sales results data is critical to both actual and predictive marketing ROI, because you can't make a calculation without a net revenues number. Without it, you'll never know the actual return on the dollars spent on your marketing investment.

Sadly, this information can be hard to pull out if your organization is sectioned into silos. Small enterprises usually can request sales data directly from the finance team, but at larger companies the marketing department may have to get it from the sales department, or request it through a senior executive to whom both departments report. In other organizations, sales data captured through customer management (CRM) databases emanates from its own silo or is part of the IT department.

The number you receive on a weekly or monthly basis may be a sales figure (gross sales) or it may be a net profit figure that takes into account cost-of-goods-sold and other depreciations. Annual figures from the finance department might be depreciated by taxes or other charges and thus be *net* income or *net* profit. While both can be used to calculate the ROI of your marketing projects, the speed of business today may suggest daily or even hourly sales figures would be handy to have. Actually, any organization that tracks sales by computer probably has the capability to review sales in real time. The bottleneck is usually the IT staff. They've got the data—ask and you may be surprised what they can access in short order.

The good news is that upper management has begun to recognize that the silo approach harms the competitive edge. In a November 2008 study by JupiterResearch and the Verse Group of over 100 U.S. marketing executives, 78 percent agreed that internal silos were the biggest barrier to integrating sales data and customer data within their organizations. In April 2009, a similar survey by the Association of National Advertisers (ANA) and 4A's (the online organ of the American Association of Advertising Agencies) of 122 in-house marketers found their greatest complaint was a lack of metrics to help them measure the effectiveness of campaigns. In this interesting study, most in-house marketers pinned the blame on "internal organizational silos" that made it difficult to collaborate. These marketers realized that funds might never be moved from legacy vehicles—newspaper ads, expensive catalogs, or sponsorships—into newer, more targeted media—mobile phone ads or e-mail—as long as sales data was unavailable and therefore could not be linked to performance.

We're constantly surprised how many marketing department staffers don't have access to revenue data in a timely fashion.

THREE "BLIND" MICE—A TRUE STORY

KG is the marketing manager of a relatively new product line that is part of a global consumer products company. As is common these days, the new product line has its own website where consumers may directly purchase any of several hundred individual stock-keeping units (SKUs) with various price points.

Her direct report, DM, is responsible for programming her line's website product offerings. With minimal guidance from KG, DM decides which of this large range of products are offered "front and center" and featured each week. She updates offerings weekly. Now this probably sounds like a lot of fun, and fairly easy—pick products, get their images and buy-page links up on the home page. But DM has no access to sales figures—she doesn't know which products are selling, which of her featured offerings are doing well, and which are not of interest to visitors to the division's website.

Sooner or later, someone in the finance silo is going to look at sales results from her division's website, and determine whether this is successful or a failure as a sales channel. This information will be given to KG, who may decide DM should be fired or replaced if the ROI derived from this channel is not in acceptable range.

DM is flying "blind"—she can change products weekly on the home page, but probably won't know if she's doing a good job until her yearly review.

KG is marketing "blind"—but she doesn't have to be. If she doesn't have daily, weekly, or monthly sales numbers for the website at her fingertips, she can get them from her website analytics report, or from senior management of her division. What good reason does she have for not sending even a summary of the data at least weekly to DM, who could then adjust product offerings to optimize the site?

The corporation is ROI "blind"—but only temporarily. At the end of the year, finance teams will look at the revenues versus expenses of online marketing for the new product line. Decisions will be made, and if the news is not good, the corporation may decide to reduce marketing budget for the new product line, or gut its web initiative.

What's really sad about the above situation is that it is all too common—many organizations hold off on reporting revenue results to their marketing staff. Much of marketing expenses tend to be annualized, and this is a trap the marketing manager needs to avoid. Too often the ROI of channel marketing campaigns and their individual initiatives is measured too infrequently, which means it may be measured inaccurately. Or the information may arrive too late to do any good. Establishing ROI for each campaign initiative is not difficult, but it's impossible if you can't get even *net revenue* data from the finance silo.

What kind of data should be asked for? At a minimum, you should get revenue numbers on a monthly basis. It takes an estimated three to six months for marketing programs to begin to produce results, and the long tail for a successful product or nonprofit program can extend years. For consumer products and to track specific campaigns, weekly or daily (for web-based businesses) data is usually available from the data silo. You just have to ask for it.

Being able to predict, or better yet show, ROI results to management on a more frequent basis is up to your needs. Having the data handy to test campaigns is seriously useful for short-term analysis. Understanding the long-term revenue results can help you better determine the success of campaigns across channels.

Sadly, this is a fairly late trend: a March 2009 survey sponsored by web agency EyeBlaster found that while 67 percent of senior marketers they polled were already doing campaigns over multiple channels, a mere 12 percent had developed the capability to integrate or measure performance across channels.

The good news is that you don't need fancy web dashboards to monitor across channels effectively. All you need is a spreadsheet program such as Excel.

Useful Tools for Budgeting, Projecting, and Tracking Expenses and ROI

One sterling example of a useful tool reported to us is a spreadsheet created by the online marketing team for the University of Pennsylvania's College of Liberal and Professional Studies distance learning programs, led by Marni Baker-Stein. Their original version mostly tracked the management investment (i.e., expenses) of their web initiatives, but even this was extensive, with separate columns for allocated overhead charges, staff time charges, and chargebacks from the university's IT staff, who managed their e-mail and CRM databases. The document also had columns to include deadlines for deliverables, launch dates, and campaign duration.

A few tweaks were all that was needed to make the document an ROI-ready spreadsheet. With the addition of columns to input revenues from students who paid for the distance learning programs (dollar figures obtained from their finance sector) the team could in fact determine ROI for a variety of marketing strategies, which ranged from banner ads to magazine print ads and e-mail blasts. Figure 2-1 shows a similar approach for a high-end consumer product marketed through an in-house e-mail list and a national magazine advertisement. Note that the formula functions within Excel can generate the mathematics for ROI percentages, by simply assigning columns to the values. How handy is that?

What we like about the University of Pennsylvania's version of the grid is that many stakeholders in the organization can view the spreadsheet and find information pertinent to them. Human resources, for example, could view the hours spent on marketing projects, and the marketing team could use the data to make the case for

Figure 2-1. Sample spreadsheet grid for tracking ROI by ad campaign and by individual media.

Product	Campaign	Initiative	Staff Time Est. ($)	Staff Time Actual ($)	Outside Services ($)	Media Buy ($)	Budget Est. ($)
Catalog AI01	Global Touch	Nat'l Mag Ad 1	$500.00	$500.00	$1,000.00	$12,000.00	$15,000.00
		Email Blast 1	$500.00	$500.00	$0.00	$0.00	$1,000.00
		Web Banner Ad	$500.00	$500.00	$1,000.00	$10,000.00	$10,000.00
		Affiliate Website 1	$200.00	$200.00	$500.00	$350.00	$1,000.00
		Affiliate Website 2	$200.00	$200.00	$500.00	$250.00	$1,000.00
		Radio Spot 1	$500.00	$500.00	$1,000.00	$7,000.00	$8,000.00
		Radio Spot 2	$500.00	$500.00	$1,000.00	$7,000.00	$8,000.00
		Facebook	$1,000.00	$1,000.00	$0.00	$2,000.00	$3,000.00
		Twitter	$1,000.00	$1,000.00	$0.00	$0.00	$1,000.00
	Totals		$4,900.00	$4,900.00	$5,000.00	$38,600.00	$48,000.00
Catalog AI02	Locial Touch	Magazine Ad 1					
		Magazine Ad 2					
		Radio Spot 3					
		Radio Spot 4					
		Facebook					
		Twitter					
	Totals						

(continues)

Figure 2-1. (Continued.)

Initiative	Actual Exp. ($)	Reach	Conversions	Conv. Rate (%)	$ Per Sale	Revenue ($)	ROI (%)
Nat'l Mag Ad 1	$13,500.00	75,000	125	0.167%	$125.00	$15,625.00	16%
Email Blast 1	$500.00	150,000	570	0.380%	$125.00	$71,250.00	14150%
Web Banner Ad	$11,500.00	250,000	25	0.010%	$125.00	$3,125.00	-73%
Affiliate Website 1	$1,050.00	500,000	35	0.007%	$125.00	$4,375.00	317%
Affiliate Website 2	$950.00	350,000	25	0.007%	$125.00	$3,125.00	229%
Radio Spot 1	$8,500.00	500,000	50	0.010%	$125.00	$6,250.00	-26%
Radio Spot 2	$8,500.00	500,000	45	0.009%	$125.00	$5,625.00	-34%
Facebook	$3,000.00	n/a	5	n/a	$125.00	$625.00	-79%
Twitter	$1,000.00	n/a	2	n/a	$125.00	$250.00	-75%
	$48,500.00	2,325,000	882	0.038%	$125.00	$110,250.00	127%
Magazine Ad 1							
Magazine Ad 2							
Radio Spot 3							
Radio Spot 4							
Facebook							
Twitter							

more staff hours to replicate projects that were proven to be revenue-enhancing. The marketing team also now has a log of what IT is charging for e-mail fulfillment, good ammo should the team wish to compare the costs for an outside e-mail fulfillment firm.

A column format like this also allows different methods for allocating overhead charges. Accounting best practices suggest that overhead be subtracted from the net revenues category rather than as part of the marketing investment. Once broken down, it can easily be shifted from one column to the next. This can be very handy when you're presenting ROI findings to upper management (see Chapter 7). For purposes of presentation, columns can of course be collapsed or hidden in Excel, depending on your audience.

The simple column format also allows room to record soft metrics, and other proxy measures of interest to the marketer but not a factor in ROI. The number of "friends" on the organization's Facebook page, the number of retweets for a viral campaign, impressions, and click-through rates can all be represented. This data allows you to seek correlations, and to determine the effectiveness of various options, such as message testing, outside of ROI.

Such simple grids can be expanded to include all that useful data from web marketing that is not ROI-related but acts as signposts to good ROI. By this, we mean the numbers you get from broader branding initiatives, which, as the decade progresses, are getting closer and closer to real ROI numbers.

At the University of Pennsylvania, the grid was so illustrative that everyone who saw it could see exactly how many students had been recruited from each of the various strategies. It was clear which programs and which initiatives were moneymakers, and which had failed to find their audience in the highly competitive space of distance learning.

Don't Drown in Data: Identify Your Most Important Metrics

Companies had so little to rely on, back in the old days, when they might spend $3 million on a television campaign, $1 million on a single 60-second Super Bowl advertisement, or—in the early stages of the web—$500,000 to purchase an AOL keyword.

In an era where even AOL has downsized—its new logo is now Aol, as if capital letters were too expensive—the one thing that just keeps getting bigger and bigger is the ability of marketers to fine-tune their measurement of return on their spending, across platforms.

Today, every movement a prospective customer makes can be tracked. Not just what happened after they clicked into the banner, entered your website, viewed a few pages, signed up as a lead, or actually purchased your product or service. Data tracking from Google and Yahoo! now allows marketers to back-track into "pre-click"—in other words, they can follow a cookie-crumb trail to *all the web pages that customer viewed prior to clicking through* to the ad. Such knowledge is indeed powerful: imagine being able to determine whether your prospective customer has been spending time on competitors' websites, glimpsed an ad in a program he or she screened at hulu.com, or spent a lunch hour at a social media website where your product or company was discussed, dissed, or enthusiastically promoted.

Much of this simply isn't being used. A barrage of surveys of traditional and web-savvy online marketers reveal that most executives routinely look at only two or three metrics: traffic, click-through rates, and dollar revenues generated at the end of a month or other sales period.

Only the dollar figures have any meaning in marketing ROI. Traffic patterns are gross indicators: the more people who arrive at an e-commerce site, the more likely people ready to buy will be among them.

Click-through rates, historically rarely greater than 0.01 percent for most online banner ad campaigns, are also gross indicators: they tell you which banners, sites, or affiliates are better at lead generation. This is related to ROI, but it's still not ROI.

But dollar figures don't lie. That's why direct response advertising vehicles remain popular, especially low-cost e-mail campaigns to accumulated lists.

All of these are costs that fall into the marketing investment portion of the ROI equation.

Quantitative Measurements Online

"We measure impressions, clicks, click-through rate, and conversion," points out web analyst Jodi McDermott, formerly at Clearspring (a cross-platform widget tools company) and now at comScore. "For brands, the value is [still] in the impression, but how does this mindset shift to valuing friends and fans or other social media actions?"

McDermott names four pay-for-performance metrics common online:

▶ Cost per click (CPC).

▶ Cost per view (CPV) for online video.

▶ Cost per install (CPI) for widgets or apps.

▶ Cost per action (CPA), which can mean the cost associated with any type of unique action that is considered a conversion.

Cost-per-click refers to what you'll pay a web affiliate, search engine, or banner ad firm each time a prospect clicks through to your home page or buy page. We wish we could say click-through rates (CTRs) are a highly accurate method of purchasing leads for your organization, but we can't. Click fraud, underattribution, and variance in results (as much as 30 percent) for even the most robust analytics programs suggest that CTRs are not accurate. Attempting to link click-through rates and what you're paying for them to ROI isn't really possible.

Cost-per-view is a popular metric now that an estimated 30 percent of the U.S. television audience is watching its Hollywood movies and mainstream TV programming—not to mention business-to-business video demos—on the web, via sites such as hulu.com, veoh.com, and YouTube. Even this top-tier programming has to share audience on digital screens (web-enabled phones, 24-inch Macintosh monitors) with the homemade videos that populate YouTube, Facebook, and other social media sites.

Advertising on all these videos is now common enough that there's even some agreement on spot length (the optimum is considered ten seconds) and what works online is being tried on broadcast and cable—including the five-second spot. But we'd argue the value of time spent watching a video has about as much value as Nielsen rating points—it's of interest, but it can't be linked to ROI on its own.

It is possible, however, to make online video advertising—or all branding efforts into a direct response medium—adding tracking tags or direct live links to a buy page. The classic success story is found in a 2009 experiment from Google, which put an ad overlay on a You-Tube video that linked to an Amazon.com buy page for DVDs of the old Monty Python movies *Life of Brian* and *The Meaning of Life*. True, this was a perfect match-up of a medium known for comic videos with a product that was comic video; according to Google, sales of both DVDs increased by 23,000 percent in the first month.

Cost-per-install became a buzzword in late 2007 when content companies first began making free widgets (small, portable applications for text, images, and audio or video clips) that could be downloaded to MySpace, Facebook, or personal web pages, and transferred peer-to-peer through e-mail. While widgets have fallen out of favor, the term lives on as the widget's successor, the downloadable "app"—again a small program, popularized by the more than 800,000 available free or cheaply for Apple's iPhone and iPad, and the newer Android phones. Other mobile devices such as the Blackberry and Barnes & Noble's Nook e-book reader all have capability for apps.

With everyone from Chanel (see Figure 2-2) to the NFL producing free or low-cost apps, this is one new wrinkle in marketing you may be asked about. Calculating cost-per-install is pretty simple, you just divide the cost of producing the app (typically $50,000 or less) by the number of downloads. This marketing investment can be calculated for ROI. While many apps are free giveaways, others are priced $.99 and up. Apple iPhone apps are just beginning to be enabled for e-commerce, but we expect to see more of this in the wake of iPad updates.

Cost-per-action is a favorite for branding expenses, but can be bent to any type of conversion. This can range from sign-ups to a newsletter or site registration (for lead generation or to create an e-mail list) to social media actions. Two such CPAs commonly tracked now are "friending" on Facebook and "following" on Twitter.

Cost-per-action can be calculated, but it's hard to link this to ROI. In discussing CPAs, McDermott notes that marketers can decide quickly how much they're willing to pay to get 5,000 "friends" on Facebook, but it's hard to determine the value of "friends."

"Getting to that ROI is not an easy problem to solve," she explains.

Figure 2-2. Chanel's app includes fashion videos and a store locator.

"In many cases you cannot, unless you are specifically tying the lifetime value of that 'friend' specifically to how much they spend with your company."

Indeed, marketers' love affair with social media may be brief, if they can't find ROI techniques in time. No one seems to want to rely on "impressions" other than to justify what may be inexpensive experiments to seem up-to-date.

Qualitative Measurements of Dubious Worth

The term "value" has been buffeted by a lot of meaning in the history of marketing. If you're in the public relations sector, you might, of old, have argued that the value of a newspaper article could be measured by the column inch, with the newspaper's ad rate providing the dollar sum for the multiplier.

That's an agency-side technique for justifying the salary of a PR person who may or may not be worth his leaded weight in newspaper leads. As we've noted, this does not become a ROI-related factor unless the article included a telephone number, and someone at the office took the calls and noted how many were for actual product orders (or dinner reservations, or sales appointments) and how many were merely congratulatory.

Business Week caused a stir this past year with a speculative article on the cash value of a Twitter "tweet"—about three cents for every thousand tweets, as based on announced deals of $25 million paid to Twitter from Google and Microsoft to make Twitter content searchable by those respective search engines. Compare this to the cost of getting a celebrity to tweet for you: the ubiquitous Kim Kardashian was reportedly paid $25,000 for a single tweet credited with driving over 40,000 visitors to an Armani website.

There has been a lot of discussion of late about how a certain number of tweets can be attributed to moving the sales needle, but it is far from an exact science at this point. If you're paying someone to tweet or manage a Facebook page for your operation, that cost naturally goes into the *marketing investment* side of your ROI equations. If you're doing this yourself, you do yourself a disservice if you do not include the value of your time (at any hourly rate) as a marketing investment spend.

Where it gets blobby is how to estimate the value of a brand-positive Twitter, Facebook, or blog mention, when the good news is coming from a brand advocate who's not on your payroll. Fortunately some good brains have been working on this one. Below is a perfect example of how a marketer can use standard formulas, such as Lifetime Customer Value, to obtain useful data from social media initiatives.

How to Derive the ROI of a Tweet Using Lifetime Customer Value

Jim Sterne is current president of the Web Analytics Association and a mastermind of social media measurement through his company, Target Marketing of Santa Barbara, California. Speaking at London's SES 2010 Conference, Sterne outlined a fairly simple way to calculate the predictive ROI value of a social media message. Using predictive ROI is perfectly fair, and it's worth a column on your ROI grid, provided you can make a good projection of a positive outcome.

In his example he used Lifetime Customer Value for a shampoo product to estimate the value of "social media participant." A participant might be a blogger, a commenter on Facebook or Twitter, or someone passing on a retweet or an RSS blog link. Assuming a new customer could provide $29 in profit for the shampoo company over a certain period in product life (let's say three years), he posited that if 10,000 participating individuals posted or passed along a message about the shampoo, and if 5 percent of them (500) actually purchased the shampoo, and five percent of those people (25) become repeat purchasers, then the value to the shampoo company of any one of the socially engaged participants would be a little over seven cents each:

$$10,000 \times 5\% = 500$$
$$500 \times 5\% = 25$$
$$25 \times \$29 = \$725$$
$$\$725 \div 10,000 = \$0.0725 \text{ per participant} = 7.25 \text{ cents}$$

If you're a seasoned marketer, the notion that 10,000 potential customers might yield twenty-five actual customers probably makes sense to you. From a predictive standpoint, paying seven cents each to gain those 10,000 potential customers would cost you $725. That's perhaps worth justifying hiring someone to blog or tweet on your behalf to try it out. To see any return on your *marketing investment* of $725, you'd have to gain at least twenty-five lifetime customers to break even on the exercise. You might be able to track it if you added a downloadable coupon or coupon code word. But if there were an alternative way to gain twenty-five (or more) new customers by spending less than $725, you'd have to compare results to see if it's really worth your time and your money.

And let's face it, this is where the sloppiness begins—the potential for large web audiences that can be as big as national television audiences used to be is something that blinds some marketers to the difficulties in really measuring impact of large-scale CPM campaigns. There are strides being made in social media measurement (see Chapter 3) but there are still pitfalls.

With that in mind, we feel the most useful qualitative measurements for marketing ROI are those that belong on the *net revenue* portion of the equation. Qualitative analysis of results, or projected results, include the following:

1. Lifetime customer value.
2. Customer acquisition cost.
3. Average purchase per visit (web or store).
4. Order value.

Let's look at these elements one at a time:

Lifetime customer value is a fairly standard calculation:

**(Average Sale) × (Average Number of Times Customers Will Reorder) =
Customer Lifetime Value**

Both figures (average sale and average reorders) can only be derived from historical data that should be made available by the sales department, finance department, or company records. If all else fails, or the venture is new, guesstimate. An average order value can be roughly determined by dividing the revenues of a given period (say a year) by the number of orders taken over the same period. Average reorders can be derived, for example, by dividing your actual total sales in a year by the number of customers you actually had in a year. To sharpen this figure further, consider removing data for your most recently acquired customers. This would leave your most loyal customers in the mix, as they are in fact the benchmark.

The resulting value of an average customer is thus useful to derive an estimate for *customer acquisition cost.*

Best practices suggest that acquisition cost estimates be based on profit, not just sales. A quick method to determine a reasonable cost to acquire a new customer is to change the first number to "average profit per sale" and then add a predetermined budget number for an acquisition cost:

**(Average Profit per Sale) × (Average Number of Times a Customer Will Reorder) +
(Amount Spent on Acquiring Customer) = Customer Acquisition Cost**

Costs to acquire vary by industry sector. The commonplace offers from banks for $50 or $100 bounties in exchange for setting up a new checking or savings account, for example, usually have a three-month period before the bounty is deposited. You may be sure all such banks have figured in how many customers will cut and run in the determination of the Lifetime Customer Value of the new customers attracted by the bounty.

Order value and average purchase per visit are hard numbers generated and viewable by most CRM data systems. The danger here is in trusting the median; you must be sure there are no anomalies, such as an extra-large purchase or seasonal surge, that are skewing the average. (See Figure 2-3 for an example that shows a typical pattern: a spike of sales on product release day, a small burst linked to a one-day sales promotion, and site traffic reflecting weekday/weekend visitors.) Many savvy organizations look at such data and divide their customers into groups based on buying behavior. Singling out high-value customers

Figure 2-3. CRM sales report showing typical pattern.

Date	Orders	Revenue	Units	Visits	Visitors	Page Views	Visitor to Order Conversion Rate
Oct 1	2,635	$105,144.00	24,241	29,722	23,570	345,959	11.18%
Oct 2	1,508	$62,970.00	13,742	26,310	21,329	274,209	7.07%
Oct 3	700	$23,901.00	5,390	16,768	13,734	174,038	5.10%
Oct 4	590	$20,100.00	4,576	16,215	13,173	157,851	4.48%
Oct 5	605	$19,690.00	4,442	23,788	19,244	210,587	3.14%
Oct 6	1,153	$37,404.00	8,041	29,166	24,093	270,249	4.79%
Oct 7	725	$22,930.00	4,912	24,306	20,080	218,742	3.61%
Oct 8	582	$17,671.00	3,803	23,831	19,588	207,294	2.97%
Oct 9	800	$27,771.00	6,183	22,785	18,868	215,332	4.24%
Oct 10	401	$11,745.00	2,594	14,500	11,968	144,868	3.35%
Oct 11	368	$11,103.00	2,430	14,146	11,764	138,525	3.13%
Oct 12	450	$13,477.00	3,034	22,108	17,941	196,842	2.51%
Oct 13	644	$18,220.00	3,962	25,563	21,093	224,558	3.05%
Oct 14	445	$12,174.00	2,758	21,504	17,877	184,188	2.49%
Oct 15	507	$14,040.00	3,122	21,767	18,104	183,921	2.80%

for special offers does not have to affect the average cost to acquire them, which can be spread out among outreach efforts to all new customers. Or not.

Fans of Pareto's Law (the well-known 80/20 rule) would do well to devise a baseline order value that can be used to compare marketing campaigns. Finding out which strategies yield the most high-value customers can help you focus your resources. But you can't assume orders are being converted through all channels at the same rate. It's hard, for example, to determine how many new sales walked in the door in response to a radio advertisement, or which came in from a flyer or billboard.

Make Sales Leads Channels Trackable

The solution to this dilemma is to make everything trackable: put a "mention this ad" action item into the radio spot or the billboard; put a scannable coupon on the flyer. Then you can use your grid to mark the conversion rate for each initiative, and track the rate against the order value and customer acquisition cost.

Businesses that rely on referrals should be able to calculate the effectiveness of their various referral programs by deploying an Order Conversion Rate either as a hard or proxy measure. In B-to-B marketing, referrals can be critical, and they must make up part of your marketing investment numbers if you are paying bounties or commissions, either formally or informally.

We've seen this done for street-level marketing, and since commissions are an allowable business tax deduction even for sole-proprietor service companies, it's normally pretty easy to get the cash figures paid out for a year or for a given month. Once you've got that number, finding the ROI for commissions you've paid is no problem at all.

TRACKING SALES LEADS: A BIG HIT ON BROADWAY

Located in the heart of Manhattan's Theatre District, PSK Consulting markets tourism services to 300 hotels through its network of concierges and other professionals in the hospitality industry. Its client lists include restaurants, nightclubs, limousine companies, and specialty tours such as the TV-themed "Sex and The City Tour," foreign-language bus and walking tours, and even a company that offers three different kinds of helicopter tours over Manhattan skies.

Hotel concierges who help tourists book a helicopter tour, for example, typically receive a commission for this referral. According to PSK principal Paul Kravitz, it's similar to the commission a tourist would pay for arranging, say, a pair of orchestra tickets to a sold-out performance of *The Lion King* or other Broadway show.

"When the customer makes a reservation for a helicopter tour, he or she pays a deposit at the hotel at the time of booking," Kravitz explained. "The customer is then given a voucher to take to the heliport, and the deposit fee is subtracted from the price of the tour."

Since the 80/20 rule applies to referrals as with any other type of sales lead, PSK Consulting—and of course the helicopter tour company—have a recurring interest in discovering which hotels provide the most referrals, and which concierges have been enthusiastic brand advocates and which may need more attention to become good advocates.

"Our system's very simple," says Kravitz. "Every hotel gets a book of vouchers, which are numbered. We know which hotel has which numbers in sequence; let's say I know 4100 to 4199 was given to a certain hotel, and this goes into the sales data." The concierge signs the voucher, which is turned in when the customer pays in full for the helicopter ride. At routine intervals, depending on the season, the vouchers are collected and matched by number to their referring hotels. ROI on the expense of the commissions may then be calculated using the receipts for the corresponding sales.

Online, the order conversion rate is often given as a percentage of traffic or unique visitors. This is an indicator, but its value to ROI calculations is dubious. Where it does have value is in the realm of site analysis—as you'd surely want to redesign your website or your marketing strategy if you got 45,000 visitors but only three purchased anything. And when expressed as a percentage, two customers with $10,000 orders are not equal to 1,000 customers with $2 orders.

Order conversion rates are also useful online if you're employing a web affiliate program.

"Share of voice," "share of wallet," "loyalty," "word of mouth," and even "engagement" can only be proxy measures. They are pointers, and you can put them on the grid if you like, but they are not ROI factors.

Revenue Side: Counting What Counts

Factors found in the net revenues portion of the ROI equation can be broken down by their revenue source. A good first step is to identify sources as individual business units, and then rename or recognize each as a "profit center." In a sales-based organization, a profit center may be an individual's sales territory, a sales region, an individual brick-and-mortar store, or a country where the sales are made for the global enterprise. A profit center can also be a specific customer market or marketplace, a specific distribution channel (online versus brick-and-mortar, online versus direct mail, catalogs versus phone or Internet sales), or a specific product line or perhaps an entire division of a larger corporation, one that has its own executive staff and marketing brand.

For the marketing manager used to "promoting the brand," the concept of breaking down marketing into specifics for different business units (profit centers) probably sounds like a lot of work. Each profit center will need its own balance sheet to measure performance, even if it's not viewed as separate by the finance department nor is separate as a legal entity for tax purposes.

Fortunately, a traditional method of tracking performance makes the process a bit more understandable. It's the old "Dupont formula"—you probably slept through it in MBA class, but to gain a more accurate picture of financial performance, Du Pont expressed ROI as equal to Total Asset Turnover times Net Profit Margin. We could really lapse into MBA-speak here, but blink your eyes to wipe off the glazing-over threat and take note that you should dig into this a bit. Just Google "Dupont formula" and you'll be led to all kinds of resources to help you narrow it down and apply it to your business. You'll learn how to calculate Total Asset Turnover (also called your Total Assets-to-Sales Ratio) and your Net Profit Margin. It's not that hard, and it's well worth the investment of time and brain cells. Here are two explanations, one from Wikipedia (http://en.wikipedia.org/wiki/DuPont_analysis) and one from Harvard (http://www.scribd.com/doc/19990953/Sustainable-Growth-Rate-and-Dupont-Analysis-Havard-Business-School).

You can use the Dupont formula for allocating assets (staff hours/payroll, dollars) to each of the strategic business units (aka profit centers) that represents each of your marketing channels or each one of your initiatives for the current season, quarter, or year.

Other Useful Operational Formulas for the Marketing Manager

Cost of goods sold (aka COGS) is a number you need to derive net revenue data. Simply, it is how much it cost to create the product or service sold. In hard goods, this includes raw materials plus manufacturing costs, as well as shipping (freight in, freight out) for raw materials and the finished product. In service industries, it is the salary cost of staff time plus their related expenses for travel, supplies, and equipment. Overhead for the organization may be included, typically as a percentage. (See the next section of this chapter.)

Inventory turnover for any goods business is also vital; marketing needs to know if product is on hand. A successful sales campaign can be a disaster if there is not enough inventory to cover a surge in demand.

For the small enterprise, here's an easy formula to discover the inventory turnover ratio:

COGS (per month) ÷ Average Inventory (per month) =
Inventory Turnover Ratio

This can also be calculated using the figures for the entire year:

COGS per year ÷ Average Inventory per year = Inventory Turnover Ratio

Note that at first glance, the numbers might seem counterintuitive: in fact, however, the lower the inventory turnover ratio, the more stock on hand. For example, as a ballpark, a turnover ratio of 12 would indicate one month's worth of inventory on hand. That's enough, perhaps, for an expected modest lift in sales. Thus, a turnover ratio of 6 would indicate two months of product is in the warehouse, which could accommodate the landslide of new and eager customers that will surely result from your new campaign. However, a turnover ratio of 25 or more is a danger sign that indicates the factory is only able to produce about two weeks' worth of inventory to accommodate its usual customers, and may have to ramp up to meet the demand of your campaign.

Will the factory be able to ship enough product to satisfy your new customers? If not, will rushed raw materials, labor overtime, and expedited shipping erode the profits from the revenues your new campaign is bringing in? These are numbers that must be factored into the COGS to get a true picture of the ROI.

This is not an idle speculation. One of the biggest disasters in online marketing history happened in 1998, the year toy retailer Toys 'R' Us launched a massive initiative for online ordering at Christmastime, promising thousands of deliveries by Christmas Day that never came through. Besides the massive loss of goodwill, the company wound up giving back several million dollars to disgruntled customers, and was subject to an FTC investigation for fraud. Today, inventory gaps are still highly publicized when they occur in consumer electronics (new phones, game consoles, e-book readers such as the Nook or Kindle), fashion (designer handbags and limited-edition cosmetics), and food. Even *The Washington Post* reported on last winter's "worldwide shortage" of Angostura Bitters created by a four-month dispute between the Trinidad manufacturer and its bottling company, and as you might imagine, food-centric bloggers had a field day with that one.

Overhead Calculation Adjustments

Marketing managers need to be familiar with the formulas used within their own organizations to calculate *overhead* if it's charged back to the marketing department and/or divided among all the marketing initiatives that you do.

Best practices again: Edward Fields, author of *The Essentials of Finance and Accounting for Nonfinancial Managers* (AMACOM Books,

2002) makes a good case for not including overhead in the operational factors for a good ROI plan, even though it's fairly routine to divide overhead by profit centers when preparing annual tax documents for the Internal Revenue Service. Fields notes: "It is presumed, incorrectly, that the methodology that must be used for regulatory compliance is also appropriate for intelligent management decision making. Nothing could be further than the truth."

The truth, Fields maintains, is that divvying up overhead burns the marketing arm of an organization in more ways than one. Burdening a new product (or a new marketing initiative) with the monkey of overhead artificially inflates the cost, making it harder to achieve break-even or profitable status. This will have the effect of strangling the new idea in its crib, once management "looks at the numbers" and decides to ax what, in the first quarter of its existence, appears to be marginal benefit to the bottom line. The incremental new business that successful marketing can achieve (tentative new customers, as opposed to active steady customers) will get swallowed up. If overhead charges are applied equally to all product lines, large and small, then the ability to provide price breaks or discounts—the heart of many promotions, online and off—is crippled, simply because the numbers won't look as good at the end of the month.

One solution for the organization is to remove overhead charges from the responsibility of individual divisions, and recognize that overall contributions to revenue are best suited to offset these charges on the general balance sheet. Otherwise, as Fields intimates, successful individual programs suffer by supporting inefficient operations at the enterprise.

A more common solution in organizations is to allocate overhead charges by percentage to each department. The percentages are created through the finance department, and probably not without a lot of internal political wrangling about what gets allotted where.

Commonly, the marketing department is given a lump sum of allotted responsibility on an annual basis. Not ideal, but common.

If your organization persists in giving the marketing department its share of the burden of overhead expenses, you, as the marketing manager, don't necessarily have to spread out that burden on to each of your initiatives, or among your various marketing channels.

With ROI in mind, remove overhead expenses from the mix, for now. Don't worry, we'll add it back later, when you'll probably need it to make a full report to your C-suite honchos. There are other, better changes to make to help you better view and improve your ROI.

CASE STUDY #2

Ice.com: Using Tweets, Blogs, and YouTube to Sell Diamonds

When asked about what he's most excited about, Pinny Gniwisch, cofounder of Ice.com, without hesitation responds, "Social media!" His years of experience developing YouTube videos, blogs, Facebook, and Twitter campaigns and more for his company have led him to the philosophy that in this socially networked world, companies must have a presence in as many places online as possible. Says Gniwisch, "Customers are out on the web experiencing countless forms of social interaction. As a company, you need to be in the medium your customers prefer to interact in. You can't afford to miss an opportunity to interact, to touch your customer."

Formed in 1999 by four ordained rabbis, Ice.com has had a storied past. Growing up working in their parents' jewelry business in Montreal, Canada, Shmuel, Mayer, and Pinny Gniwisch and their brother-in-law Moshe Krasnanski knew they could leverage that experience and associated connections in an online venture. Formed originally as Buyjewel.com, they became part of Bill Gross's Idealab Internet retail incubator in Pasadena, California. At the time, Gross had visions of aggregating a number of Internet retail operations under one brand, Big.com, and going head-to-head with Amazon.com. By October 2000, with the dotcom crash still ringing in everyone's ears, Idealab's roll-up of online retailers was falling apart. The brothers were able to negotiate a buyback of their company, now with the new domain name Ice.com, from Gross for its debt, or about $600,000.

Moving back to Montreal, the company soon reached break-even and has been building from there. The company has raised two rounds of venture funding and has bought an online rival, Diamond.com, which sells slightly higher end jewelry. The acquisition currently represents about a third of their business.

Faced with a crowded marketplace and difficulty differentiating themselves in customers' eyes, the company embarked on its first social media initiative in 2006. Sticking to the web axiom of "tell me, don't sell me" the blogs focus on being very editorial, not commercial. The company's first blog, "Sparkle Like the Stars," is written in two different voices created by one writer. One was a flamboyant designer and the other a star-struck young girl obsessed with celebrity watching—and with the jewelry film and TV stars prefer. "We will write stories about jewelry being worn by celebrities at awards shows like the Grammys or Oscars, and mention products that we carry that can help our customers get the same effect," explains Gniwisch.

After the initial success of "Sparkle Like the Stars," Ice.com started another blog, "Just Ask Leslie," which focuses on providing tips and answering questions about jewelry care and style. "Customers were asking us questions about jewelry suggestions for a certain dress or event that didn't necessarily fit in our FAQs (frequently asked questions) on our website, so the 'Just Ask Leslie' blog was created to handle them and broadcast them to a larger audience."

Their blogs receive 15,000–20,000 unique visitors per week, so they work hard to keep the content fresh and exciting. The company has people dedicated to blogging and tweeting, and in the past year can specifically track more than $100,000 in sales coming from their blogs.

After the blog success, the company moved to YouTube, producing videos relating to Valentine's Day and Mother's Day. Categorized as "Pinnysworld," the videos simply show Pinny Gniwisch stopping passersby and asking them questions about gift giving or other topics (for entertainment purposes) as they present themselves. The promotion of Ice.com may come as a scroll across the bottom of the screen, a banner at the end, or an entertaining spokesperson at the end imploring viewers to visit Ice.com.

Besides sales, Gniwisch can directly attribute customer acquisition stats to these social networking efforts. "Our video views, which total about a quarter of a million, have led to 6,500 people signing up for our mailing list, agreeing to receive promotional offers and other information from us."

Blog entries, tweets, and videos can all be measured. Taking a page from direct marketing, where 800 numbers are individualized to specific messages, campaigns, and/or markets, or URLs are modified slightly in infomercials and direct response commercials for similar reasons, Ice.com uses unique URLs in their posts. This way, there is not just a simple, anecdotal rationalization that their social media work is paying off, they know most certainly that "Tweets lead to sales."

Yet in the midst of experimentation, Ice.com maintains web fundamentals to constantly improve the customer experience. By watching reviews of their products and shopping experience online, and by monitoring Facebook, Twitter, and the feedback their customer service reps were getting, the company was able to determine that the static images, the product shots of jewelry on their website, left much to be desired. The size of the stones in the rings, the sparkle, the color, or the clarity of the diamonds was not translating well to the still image. This led the company to begin experimenting with providing videos of their products. The products are shot on a model, as well as rotating on a carousel to provide plenty of sparkle opportunity and provide the customer with a better sense of scale of the piece. One result: Product returns have dropped from 12 percent to 9 percent. Seeing the item "in context" allowed the customer to more accurately envision how the piece of jewelry would look.

"When we tested the pages where products were shown in a video versus being displayed as static images, the conversion rate for the products purchased after viewing the video jumped 400 percent," relates Gniwisch. The company is in the process of providing video images of all of its products, replacing the static images. The videos are short fifteen-second segments that are to the point, providing multiple product shots and a nice, professional voiceover. Besides the video, product pages were redesigned to showcase the video at the top of each page. Customer reviews and a "Buy Now" button are also prominently displayed.

Ice.com has also discovered the benefits of engaging with their customers. "Social media gives us lots of opportunities to nip problems in the bud. If we see a customer blogging or tweeting about a bad experience with Ice.com, we work diligently to engage in a conversation with that customer. We will identify what their specific problem is, and let them know what we'll do to address their issue," explains Gniwisch. This has led to customers retracting and even removing negative tweets from their Twitter feed and instead posting positive reviews and raves about their customer experience.

Importantly, engaging customers online means more than simply monitoring Twitter and Facebook to address complaints. The company launched a campaign for Mother's Day 2009, asking readers to send in their favorite breast cancer story. "We were expecting about 150 stories." They publicized the story campaign on their blogs, tweets, and their home page. When the final tally was done, the company received 6,800 breast cancer stories. "We were blown away by the response. Our customers had so many things to tell us!"

In a recent radio interview he summarizes why he believes in multiple touch points for customers and the power of social media to ROI:

"I call it the beehive effect. Bees represent our customers, and each day they go out and look for flowers to land on and sample the nectar. These flowers all over the place are equal. No flower can scream louder than the next. The bee sort of senses which one it'll go to, the best one. Now, depending how many flowers you have out there, where flowers represent destinations, more bees will have access to your company. So let's say if one flower represents Facebook, one flower represents YouTube, one flower represents blogs, you have all of these opportunities to touch a customer. In the new marketing world [it] will be about touch points. [Through] how many touch points will your customer be able to touch your company.

"You cannot necessarily measure the immediate effect when someone watches your video and comments about it to a friend, you don't know what happens after that. But, it is another touch point. It's like a halo effect when your customers have multiple opportunities to meet you, to greet you, in all of these online interactions. It's like recency and frequency in radio advertising. Being in multiple places in the social media space enables you to remain top of mind with your customer."

Measuring the Immeasurable

Branding, Buzz, and Social Media

ONE OF THE FIERCEST BATTLES in marketing today is whether or not the traditional methods to put value on mass media are still relevant when we talk about the economics of ROI. Two philosophies have emerged.

The first one attempts to apply, or at least retrofit, the older measurement systems created for print, radio, and TV, such as CPM (cost per thousand) and GRP (gross rating points), to gain some insights into the value of investing marketing dollars in derivative media such as web video or the online version of an industry or consumer magazine. This can work if the communication is a true form of mass communication—a branded, deliberate message from the company to large numbers of customers at the same time.

The second philosophical approach looks at new and different ways to measure the value of branding messages for new forms of communication. Blogs, Twitter, Facebook, and the like can command the audience of a mass medium, yet by their nature are closer to old-fashioned word of mouth. More rightly they may be called peer-to-peer communication, because these channels facilitate an unmediated conversation that is horizontal (customer to customer) and exponential (you tell/tweet two friends, they tell/tweet two friends, etc.). Calculating the result of a peer-to-peer snowball effect is difficult; predicting a likely result is even harder.

This chapter looks at both methods to help you examine comparatives for your *marketing investment* in branded messaging. But don't worry—we'll also give you a few solid techniques for measuring their ROI.

Brand Spending Revisited

Reach, frequency, brand recall, ad recall, purchase intent—all these fuzzy metrics for print, radio, and television should have fallen by the wayside a decade ago.

These measures haven't gone away because there has been no other definitive way to measure the equally fuzzy impact of a TV or radio commercial, a billboard, or merely the mention of a product or name upon consumer behavior. Broadly, it's possible to correlate reach and frequency of ad message to sales: a nationally shown TV commercial for a new product will eventually move product, if no one had ever heard of it before the message aired. Yet a single 140-character tweet can do the same, at a microscopic fraction of the cost. In this context, does CPM really matter?

Let's take a look at some old measurements and how they hold up now. As in the old days, CPM is not a measurement of your marketing ROI, or your skill in wringing another 15 percent discount off a magazine's advertising rate card. Its use lies in *calculating your marketing expense*. That's half the ROI equation, so that's where the worth is.

So, let's look at CPM: it's used for direct mail (and for e-mail) as well as for print advertising. In the print world, there is no true CPM. Your dollar cost "per thousand" subscribers always was a bogus number. Your "controlled-circulation" trade publication promised to deliver 40,000 executive addresses; presumably the magazine got mailed, then arrived; perhaps the executives were too busy to read them so they wound up in the lobby and were swiped by job prospect interviewees. (So much for "passalong"—right?) Even consumers who *pay* to receive magazines and newspapers often don't read them, although the odds are greater they will if they are young and/or female. And if they've paid for them—which is not the case for controlled-circulation magazines that offer subscriptions for free.

Online, the formulas for calculating CPM are even more imaginary: e-mail lists not purged or updated are near useless for targeted marketing, unless you're the rare purveyor of Viagra at rock-bottom prices. Online publications may try to pitch you CPM for banner ad space, based on traffic levels. Even if traffic levels are observed by an independent entity (such as comScore or MinOnline.com, which specializes in tracking traffic on websites owned by consumer and B-to-B magazines), there is no guarantee that your message is getting adequate exposure—a message placed low down on a web page may be invisible to 30 percent of viewers who can't be bothered to scroll down.

The click-through rate (CTR), a metric that endures because of its usefulness in search marketing, is often applied to branding message purchases, either by CPM or on a performance basis. While myriad factors can skew click-through data, any ratio that is 0.10 percent (yes, a mere tenth of a percent) or greater for a branding banner is the equivalent of a major league baseball hitter's .300 average. But we'd suggest you just fix in mind that all you'll get is a mildly interested prospect, not a potential customer, out of every 100 clicks, and you'll be well on your way to rational online CPM. You'll get a clearer picture (no pun intended) for CPMs purchased for online video, with some new data sources such as comScore's Videometrix 2.0 (www .videometrix2.com), which separates out ad viewing from content viewing and counts actual reach of ads delivered and what percentage were viewed in their entirety.

And none too soon. The most recent statistics on web advertising by eMarketer found that of the $25 billion spent on online ads each year, only $7.7 billion—roughly a third—was allocated to branding ads (banners and video). Much of the rest is still spent on search marketing, which has adapted the methods of direct response marketing and returns what are considered fairly reliable numbers for ROI.

"But unlike search, which is a $12 billion business, we don't know what that $7.7 billion is doing for us," explains Geoff Ramsey, CEO of eMarketer. "If we figure it out, that number will grow. Search and online video are the two engines driving Internet growth, and search has slowed. We really have to figure out the branding component and apply to online video or we will be stagnant."

Online Branding: Where Does It Fit?

The most important innovation that has been brought to marketing from Internet disciplines is the incorporation of trackable methods of

Figure 3-1. Where online ad money is spent.

U.S. Online Ad Spending by Format, 2006–2011	2006	2007	2008	2009	2010	2011
Paid Search	40.3%	40.3%	40%	39.8%	39.8%	39.5%
Display Ads	21.8%	21.9%	21.5%	20.5%	20%	19.5%
Classifieds	18.1%	17%	17%	16.9%	16.8%	16.5%
Rich Media/Video	7.1%	8.2%	9.5%	11.%	11.9%	13.1%
Paid Referrals	7.8%	8.1%	8.3%	8.6%	8.8%	8.8%
E-mail	2.0%	2.0%	1.8%	1.7%	1.6%	1.5%
Sponsorships	2.9%	2.5%	2.0%	1.5%	1.3%	1.2%
Total (Billions)	$16.9	$21.4	$27.5	$32.5	$37.5	$42

Source: eMarketer

linking branding advertisements to direct response and into the sales funnel. This revelation, as early as 2006, came from research that found adding display ads on the web increases search activity. In light of the dollars and the credibility web marketers give to search, the mere fact that sales could in any way be attributed to good effects of branding ads on the web wasn't just a shot in the arm to marketers weary of click-through rates below a tenth of one percent. In short, it signaled the idea that legacy branding initiatives might be trackable enough to be evaluated for their return on investment, if some signal could be transmitted through the sales funnel.

Online, the lift from branding into direct response seems to be a reliable 20 percent, although not for all industry categories. A survey from Specific Media found that display is most helpful for products that are best researched on the Internet: travel, health, personal finance, news, and real estate (see Figure 3-2). In this study, the increase in productive click-throughs for these categories averaged 155 percent. Consumer products and retailers saw much more modest lift, with packaged goods closer to the 20 percent average.

This is in line with a general theory that branding works best

Figure 3-2. Online display boosts search activity.

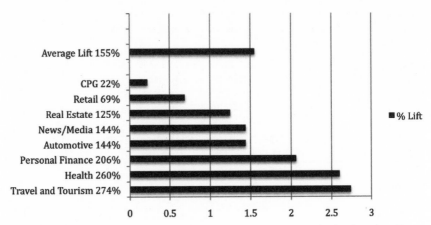

Note: *among Specific Media clients; **ad-exposed consumers who searched on brand and/or segment-related terms vs. unexposed consumers
Source: Specific Media as cited in press release, December 3, 2008

when the path to purchase is longer and subject to serious consideration by the end consumer. Historically, branding advertisements have been shown to assist major purchases, such as automobiles, appliances, and expensive electronics equipment. In past years, a prospective purchaser might peruse magazine articles or poll peers for a length of time while simultaneously being bombarded with brand advertising for the object in question.

"People don't just see an ad or billboard and do something immediately—it happens over time," notes eMarketer Geoff Ramsey. This provides a rationale for branding on the web, if your target audience attends to web media more than magazines or television.

Both Yahoo! and comScore have presented deeper studies evaluating the lift display ads give to online searches that can be directly attributed to consumer buying behavior (see Figures 3-3 and 3-4). In this test, web display ads improved online sales by 42 percent, while search alone improved sales by 121 percent (over a control group). But online sales among customers who could be tracked to both a web display ad and a search activity were improved by 178 percent.

ComScore also looked at the dollars generated by each of the three strategies, making it possible for the companies involved to calculate not just comparative lift, but comparative ROI.

Two earlier studies from Yahoo! and comScore, one in 2008 and

Figure 3-3. Percent of Internet users making an online purchase after ad exposure.

Percent of US Internet Users Who Make on Online Purchase on the Advertiser Site After Being Exposed to Online Display and/or Search Ads, 2008

	Control	Test	Lift
Display only	1.0%	1.5%	42%
Search only	1.1%	2.4%	121%
Search and display	1.9%	5.1%	173%

Note: home, work, and university locations; retail sites only
Source: comScore Brand Metrix, "How Online Advertising Works: Whither the Click," December 5, 2008

Figure 3-4. Dollars spent by Internet users making an online purchase after ad exposure.

Online Retail Sales* from US Internet Users Exposed to Online Display and/or Search Ads, 2008

	Control	Test	Lift
Display only	$ 994	$1,263	27%
Search only	$1,548	$2,724	76%
Search and display	$2,723	$6,107	124%

Note: home, work, and university locations, *monthly sales per thousand exposed consumers ranging from two weeks to three months after the initial exposure
Source: comScore Brand Metrix, "How Online Advertising Works: Whither the Click," December 5, 2008

one in 2007, also found convincing evidence that web display ads, in combination with search, can boost offline, brick-and-mortar retail sales and increase store visits. Thus, web-influenced, cross-channel marketing messages are being employed more vigorously to get customers into shops and not just shopping online.

Ironically, one of the first victories, reported in *The Wall Street Journal*, came from Chrysler. Their agency, Organic (a division of Omnicom), used attribution modeling to track response from TV ads to a website for prospective car buyers. Not only did the agency learn which ads prompted more visits to the website, they also discovered which online activities were most predictive of an actual purchase. One of the top predictors was entering a zip code to locate the nearest Chrysler dealer, and in one initiative, for the Jeep brand, the results predicted 2008 sales within one percentage point of actual sales figures for the brand!

We've also seen some interesting developments in correlating cross-channel branding with sales data. Nielsen's Homescan unit, in cooperation with Yahoo!, tracks online ad exposures among panels of shoppers. In December 2009 Nielsen took another step, with Nielsen Catalina Ventures, to create what they bill as the first "TV return on investment measurement service" using data from the same Homescan box, to correlate TV watching behaviors with Internet use and purchase data from an estimated 50 million shoppers who receive print marketing materials through Catalina Marketing's retailer network.

If it seems we have digressed here, it is because the majority of marketers who think they are measuring branding are measuring the wrong things. Several surveys from *PROMO Magazine* of their readership, which is primarily direct-response marketers, show that more than half of these ROI-savvy executives are still relying on click-through rates as their primary metric for brand effectiveness, and only a third even bother to measure the ROI of their promo initiatives.

Brand veterans such as Gian Fulgoni, chairman of independent rating service comScore, support the notion that branding efforts may be undervalued in an industry leaning heavily to direct response. The comScore white paper, "How Online Advertising Works: Whither the Click?" (also published in the *Journal of Advertising Research* on June 15, 2009) is worth reading (www.comscore.com/request/whither-the-click.asp). The team looked at 200 cross-media studies to conclude that an ad impression on the Internet works just like an ad impression in traditional media, and that reach and frequency are useful to know, if not inherently measurable. The same frustrations rule: advertisers still find measuring systems inadequate, and media outlets continue to fear that their placements are undervalued.

Web Video Advertising and Ratings: Gross but to the Point

There was probably some dancing in the conference rooms of major advertising agencies when it was discovered that marketing clients could be suckered—ahem, we mean "enlightened"—into the notion that gross ratings points (GRPs) were a valid and trackable way to evaluate the costs of advertising during an online video program. This after many years of ratings companies and ad agencies assuring their clients that video downloads weren't really stealing audience from network, cable, and local television fare.

By 2009 there was undisputed proof that a good 60 percent of television watching—be it sports programming, movies, or the latest episode of *The Simpsons*—was being done on a computer screen. The ratio was even greater for the most desirable demographic of young men (aged 18–24), so 2009 was the year web video advertising came of age. Many experiments were tried: pre-roll, post-roll, different lengths, interstitial, sponsored, use of motion video, static and animated banners that accompanied the content on other parts of the viewing screen, and more.

How have major U.S. advertisers adapted? For starters, costs of advertising are now amortized to include web viewing, as favorite ads can be archived on your web site, or, if truly popular, will surface on YouTube in fan postings or passalongs. Creating advertising that appears online is either a new expense or is financed by shifting funds from broadcast/cable purchasing.

And how is the ROI calculated on this spending? You could try GRPs, which have been used for television advertising since the days of the dinosaurs (or at least *The Flintstones*). This old soft metric is a measurement of ad "impressions" by television viewers. Like CPM, it estimates how many people *might* have had the opportunity to see and hear your message. Don't think of it in the old terms of "reach" and "frequency." It is a way to reimagine and give some numerical value to the unknowable audience that you have at least the potential to reach online.

Josh Chasin, the chief research officer for comScore, has argued that GRPs can be used to evaluate web video advertising, and even other forms of web advertising, such as banners on a blog, content site, or Facebook page. In a May 2010 article for *MediaPost*, he outlined both the history and the future he sees for GRPs in marketing.

"When media choices were limited and broadcast advertising was new, no one thought about moving beyond the GRP metric; you simply bought a ton of advertising, and it worked," Chasin says. "And if it didn't work, you fired the agency. GRPs were, and are, a measure of tonnage."

Unlike click-through rates, which can be evaluated to a specific message event online (a banner appears on X day on X web page), gross rating points measure the accumulated exposure of multiple events to an audience that's been estimated as a percentage of the potential audience overall.

Because GRPs are the sum of the ratings of all events associated with an advertisement (i.e., ratings for all the programs the ads ran in), Chasin points out that this multi-point ability makes GRPs applicable and in fact ideal for evaluating commercial ad buys on web video, because the events can be scattered (hundreds or thousands of viewings of the program over any period of time, not just an initial telecast) but are still countable, because downloads and completed viewings can be counted quite easily.

But Chasin goes even further: if visits to web media that are not clickable can still be counted as "impressions," delivered on a one-by-one basis to a computer user who surfs a web page, then GRPs can measure impressions and perhaps their relative value as well.

The real key to GRP, says Chasin, is that ratings can be expressed in terms of a population, not just a program. This makes it a cross-platform metric that he envisions could be applied to any media channel, not just the website traffic channels that comScore has tracked for years.

"The population doesn't change across media—there are 300 million people in the U.S., regardless of whether you work in TV, radio, print, or digital," he explains. "Here's another fact about GRPs that you need to know: 100 GRPs is equivalent to the number of impressions you need to reach everyone in the population at one time. . . . [Television] ratings are percentages against the population, and GRPs [are] the individual ratings summed up.

"So if your digital target is women 18–34, and you know you bought 26 million impressions against that target online, then guess what? Since the population is known—about 35 million women are 18–34 in the U.S.—you've just bought yourself 74 GRPs of Women 18–34.

Here's Chasin's calculation for deriving GRPs from any impressions buy online: impressions divided by population, then multiplied by 100 to find the percentage. That is,

$$\text{Impressions} \div \text{Total Population} \times 100 = \text{GRP}$$

We would agree that to make this most useful you must recognize the entire population for any form of media—of the city, the country, or the world. Limiting the population to only Internet users, or only an estimated number of iPhone users, skews the reach unfairly. That was the mistake television ratings agencies and ad agencies made when computer screens began to lure viewers away from the living room TV set. They ignored these new screens and relied on old set-top metering boxes, which no longer gave a true picture of reach or potential audience.

GRP used as Chasin suggests also solves a problem marketers have had in measuring branding: because GRP represents the sum of many events, the math is flexible enough to accommodate the longer periods of time a signature branding message might run.

So can this apply to all forms of branding? And all forms online?

"The question of whether GRPs are a relevant metric online is simply the wrong question," says Chasin. "As long as you know how many impressions you bought against a target, and how many people comprise that target, your GRPs are, a priori, *known* . . . a known, fundamental, derivative measure of the tonnage of advertising bought, and the metric allows that tonnage to be compared across media: 'I bought 200 GRPs of TV and 75 GRPs online.'"

In the ROI grid, GRPs can be a soft metric for comparing one or two ad channels in the *marketing expense* half of your ROI equation. Matching GRPs directly to ROI is possible if you can obtain sales data before, during, and after the life of a branding campaign.

There are a slew of other statistics that some ad agencies like to trumpet to get your attention. These are "brand awareness" statistics. Ad recall, intent to purchase, like/dislike, preference, would recommend, etc., are the stuff generated out of panels, online marketing questionnaires, focus groups, and the like. Of these, only one factor has proven to be a reliable measure of future sales—"would recommend."

Customers who would recommend your product or service to a friend or colleague are potential brand advocates and can be your valuable allies in word-of-mouth advertising. That's the kind of buzz that money can't buy. Unless, of course, you're investing marketing dollars into the latest buzz craze: social media.

ABCs OF GRPs

Gross rating points originated in broadcast media. First radio, and then television, had audiences measured at the program level: how many listeners or viewers were in the audience for a specific show? The result was a program rating. On January 19, 1953, for example, for the episode "Lucy Goes to the Hospital," *I Love Lucy* garnered a 72 household rating—72 percent of all TV households in the United States were tuned to the program (at least, according to Nielsen).

Advertisers, of course, ran schedules, which were simply collections of spots. Each spot ran in a program, and so could be associated with that program's audience rating. The GRP emerged as a way to express the audience to an aggregate of spots, which is to say a schedule, and its calculation couldn't have been more simple: the sum of the program ratings for all the spots in the schedule. If an advertiser bought ten spots across ten different programs, and each program had a rating of 7, then the gross rating points—the sum of the ratings of the spots in the schedule—would be 70. If an advertiser had run two spots in that landmark episode of I Love Lucy, they would have bought 144 GRPs (which would be parsed as a reach of 72, with a frequency of 2.)

Over time, broadcast audience measurement got more granular. In the sixties, household ratings gave way to demographic person ratings. Program ratings were replaced by average quarter-hour ratings (how many people were in the audience during the average 15-minute period) and ultimately, for network TV, by average minute ratings. The idea of moving beyond the program rating to the average minute rating was to make the audience estimate approximate as closely as possible the potential reach of an actual commercial: if 20 million people watched a program at some point during the hour it aired, but in an average minute only 15 million were watching, then 15 million was a better estimate of the audience an advertiser could reach with a single commercial.

—Josh Chasin, comScore

Brand Measurements and Buzz: Social Media

Online, the battle over how to value branding measures has nearly been won. This came about as soon as online marketers began to adapt the techniques of search to display advertising and even video advertising on the web.

What's holding it back? True measurement of online branding includes the proliferation of other things that are countable. Rather than searching for true ROI, purveyors of media have an incentive to count that which is easy to measure. For online video these countable items may be downloads or completed plays. For social media it may be the number of fans, friends, or followers. These are sometimes thought to be measures of "engagement" or interactivity. But they are at best directional.

How do you measure online buzz? Some of the greatest minds in twenty-first-century marketing have pondered this question, and in polling them all for practical advice we have determined you have four choices when deciding how and with what resources you will measure the ROI of your social media initiatives. Because even if your organization isn't heavily active in online social media now, or if your CEO/CFO still thinks it's simply a fad, you will eventually be using these communications tools, either in your current job or your next one. Your choices:

Strategy #1: Don't bother to measure it: let it flow.

Strategy #2: Give responsibility (and budget) to public relations staff.

Strategy #3: Make every social media outreach trackable to ROI.

Strategy #4: Measure everything you can measure, but as proxy only.

All of these are valid approaches to finding ROI in social media. Let's look at each of them.

Strategy #1: Don't Bother to Measure It: Let It Flow

According to a September 2009 study of global marketers, less than 20 percent of these best-in-class companies measure the ROI of their social media outreach on outlets such as Twitter, FriendFeed, YouTube, Facebook, LinkedIn, Squidoo, or Foursquare. Major advertisers are understandably uncomfortable with social media—they have no control over what people say about them, online or off, and typically are not nimble enough to match the speed of word-of-mouth or word-of-web conversations that can make or break a product in the public eye.

Steve Woodruff is a longtime web consultant to the pharmaceutical industry—one of the biggest spenders of branding dollars. Speaking recently as the founder and president of Impactiviti (www.impactiviti.com), he has identified four reasons why many large firms shy away from reporting ROI results from social media, and one reason more for why others are just waiting it out.

"Doing simplistic ROI for social media is putting square pegs into round holes," he declares. "Social media is serendipitous, it's holistic, and it's not linear. It can't be planned. And, it's not long-term enough for measurement."

Woodruff notes corporations have jumped the gun on ROI measurements for developments that, like social media, may eventually drastically change corporate behaviors. "Does anyone remember the ROI of giving computers to employees?" he asks. "That was a big question if you do remember it—who in the organization would get a computer? Who really needed one enough to justify the cost? And we don't ask that question anymore." The notion that social media isn't the flavor of the month in marketing (anyone remember Second Life?) but a significant step in communications that bears watching is shared by many veteran marketers willing to experiment for now.

Historically, word-of-mouth advertising has no ROI. While seeds can be planted for conversations, there is no control over how the public views your organization. Peer-to-peer communication just flowed, when it was just people talking. What changed the game is that peer-to-peer conversations on the web are easily recorded and can remain in online archives in transmittable forms—perpetuating brand perceptions, good or bad, to successive waves of peers.

Strategy #2: Give Responsibility (and Budget) to Public Relations Staff

For many types of companies, the entry level to social media has not been conversation, but observation. Best-in-class companies such as Ford, IBM, and American Express all employ teams that monitor large chatter streams on Facebook and Twitter as well as blogs and online bulletin boards that discuss their services and praise or complain about products, sales support, or company practices.

Tracking and helping to direct public conversations about the organization has long been the turf of the corporate public relations department, either in-house or outsourced to a public relations professional. Does social media belong to the PR team? If so, then efforts may not be subject to ROI, and expenses not taken out of the marketing budget. If you are in charge of the PR budget, the decision to measure the ROI of your social media outreach is up to you. What's more important: Which segment of the organization *has the resources* to devote to "listening" to web conversations? Which segment of the organization is responsible for correcting erroneous information circulating through rumor and retweets? Who controls brand management? If this is out of your control, consider relinquishing social media and its ROI until it is.

A mid-sized company has the choice of hiring staff to monitor web chat or hiring a listening company. These service firms will comb the net for mentions of your firm or product or particular key words that are key to your industry.

Key players in the listening game are Synthesio, Radian6, Brand-Watch, and Sysomos—though there are many more. SAS, well known for its sales platforms, has also introduced a semantic analysis product. Monitoring is done either in automated fashion, or by human beings who hunt for keywords on a 24/7 basis. Companies use a variety of programs known as *sentiment analysis* to tell you if comments about your company are favorable, unfavorable, or neutral. While you'll find no shortage of firms offering sentiment analysis, interpretation is still somewhat shaky at the moment.

The smallest companies can also do some adequate monitoring of their brand through free or low-cost tools. GoogleAlerts is a free service (www.google.com/alerts) that returns to you a daily digest of URLs that have mentioned your company or product—or any topic that may be trending or of interest to you. It allows you to monitor your firm's reputation online and even covers Facebook and LinkedIn, which allow you to see if your account exec is actively job-hunting, and help you decide whether you should ask Susie from accounting to take down that photo of her doing the limbo a bit low at the company Christmas party.

Socialmention (www.socialmention.com) offers free basic tools for tracking mentions of topics or companies (yours or a competitor's) over 100 social networks, including FriendFeed, Digg, YouTube, Google, Twitter, and Facebook.

To get a handle on how much tracking governance is needed, consider going to Twitter and typing in your company or product name; you'll get real-time results going back a week or more. The company, based in San Francisco, offers insights on how to use this data at: http://business.twitter.com/twitter101/.

As long as you're not attempting to tie word-of-mouth to ROI, social media can reside as a soft metric in your ROI grid, along with other indicators such as estimated reach or frequency rates for an ad buy. And social media outreach may be comfortably allotted to the public relations team for more than just monitoring. Brand messaging without a hard sell, and without attendant ROI requirements, can help develop brand advocates among your customer base. Remember the "recommend" factor? One thing that social media outreach can do is to identify strong advocates for your brand; and once identified, they could be contacted for later roles in more results-oriented marketing efforts. This is easier than ever on the Internet, with online tools available from socialmention.com and Technorati.com, to name but a few.

In fact, locating web "influentials" is considered so important to brand marketing that even the Federal Trade Commission keeps an eye on it. Bloggers and tweeters who give endorsements or are given products to review are now required to state what's been given and who solicited the endorsement. The official guidelines are here: http://www.ftc.gov/multimedia/video/business/endorsement-guides.shtm.

SOCIAL STATS WORTH TRACKING

Here are some simple, countable statistics that you or your PR staff can use to create "snapshots" of online buzz:

- ▶ *Company blog:* Page visits, return visits, number of inbound links from other blogs.
- ▶ *Independent blogs:* Number of mentions that include site links to your website.
- ▶ *Facebook:* Page visits, return visits, number of fans for corporate or product page.
- ▶ *Twitter:* Retweets of a company tweet message by others.
- ▶ *YouTube:* For individual videos, views; for multiple videos, visits to corporate channel.
- ▶ *Widgets or Apps hosted on third-party sites:* Number of downloads.

Strategy #3: Make Every Social Media Outreach Event Trackable to ROI

It's entirely possible to make every corporate tweet, every bulletin board submission, and every Facebook update trackable and clickable—just add a link or URL to make the offer actionable and offer something of value or a treat. This can be a downloadable coupon, a secret coupon code for a special discount, free content in the form of a widget, useful application, industry sales report, or cool video—even a passalong joke or a photo that's been tagged so it can be counted.

Retailers get the most use out of this. Old Navy's Facebook fan page boasts over 500,000 "friends." The department store Macy's has about 400,000. These fashion purveyors keep potential customers coming back with several tempting offers each day. The majority of postings relate to a specific product SKU that may be purchased in-store or online; other postings lead readers to website activities such as games, contests, sweepstakes, and tie-ins with celebrity promotions that involve print and television. Staples, the office-supply chain, has five full-time staffers creating SKU-based promotions on Twitter alone. But how can their success be measured?

One of the earliest successes on Twitter has been that of Dunkin' Donuts, the coffee chain. The promotion was "Win Free Coffee for a Year" and the role of "Chief Tweeter" was given to marketing exec David Puner. His tweets are typical—140-character notices of special deals or contests, answers to queries, and frequent invitations to join a special "DD Perks" by sign-up. Users who sign up are entered into a company database; the company assigned a *quantitative value* for database members. This group of opt-in fans could be given special offers, which were then trackable to ROI when the offers were redeemed at local stores.

Strategy #4: Measure Everything That Can Be Measured, but as Proxy Only

To make all of your social media trackable misses the whole point of social media: it's a conversation, not a variant of an e-mail blast. Communication in the social space is best used to extend brand awareness, foster brand advocacy, build a fan base, and build your brand. Forget the hard sell—use the channel to build community around your organization.

This notion goes back to the earlier web functions of community bulletin boards—as far back as the late 1980s. The best practices that worked then still work now. Allow peer-to-peer communication to happen around you, and use the conversation for feedback. Sit on your hands, lurk, and listen, and refrain from responding to pans and punches. Most of all, when you do post, always give folks stuff to talk about.

Two good examples here: Tiffany & Co., the high-end jewelry retailer, has 300,000 followers on Facebook. They do push new products, but you'll never see a coupon code promotion here. Instead, the daily feeds show celebrities decked out in jewels, and offer tips for gift giving in season.

Wal-Mart, the department store chain, has taken its lumps in social media—but it's still brave enough to let the conversation flow. In early 2010, the biggest conversation wasn't even on Wal-Mart's official fan page; Wal-Mart doesn't have one. Instead, the buzz was on a renegade page called "Screwing Around in Wal-Mart"—devoted to postings that showed people running around the store, playing games with the sports equipment, eluding the security guards, and acting in infantile ways. Some 236,000 followers comment and post on the antics. A link to the chain's website is prominent, and the message is clear: Wal-Mart is a fun place to visit. As far as getting young, dis-affected, surly post-teens into the stores, it's a brilliant concept, no matter whose idea it was at first. Small wonder the corporation is hands-off as far as conversation is concerned. But you can bet they are monitoring this 24/7.

David Berkowitz, Senior Director of Emerging Media for agency 360i, came up with a list last fall of "100 Ways to Measure Social Media." We think it's instructive and reprint part of it here:

SELECTION FROM "100 WAYS TO MEASURE SOCIAL MEDIA"

11. Mainstream media mentions
12. Fans
13. Followers
14. Friends
15. Growth rate of fans, followers, and friends
16. Rate of virality/passalong
17. Change in virality rates over time
18. Second-degree reach (connections to fans, followers, and friends exposed—by people or impressions)
19. Embeds/installs
20. Downloads
21. Uploads
22. User-initiated views (e.g., for videos)
23. Ratio of embeds or favoriting to views
24. Likes/favorites
25. Comments

—From "100 Ways to Measure Social Media" by David Berkowitz. Used by permission.

Berkowitz's point is that studying buzz is really getting out of hand.

What may be more useful, however, is his proposal for an additional pricing model that could be useful for ROI calculations. He calls this CPSA, or cost-per-social-action, which may theoretically be applied to the costs that fall under the marketing investment part of the ROI equation.

Broadly described, the actions to be measured in CPSA consist of "any action with a distinctly social quality that leads to either new relationships (such as viral referrals or acquiring new followers or fans) or deepening existing relationships." Actions considered to deepen relationships would include a user making a comment, writing a review, or promoting someone else's comment on a social site. The cost for the action might be the money lost on a discounted coupon, or it could simply be the cost of the human monitoring and updating social media postings for your company. When such postings result in comments, a comment can be counted as a CPSA.

Says Berkowitz: "The main benefit of CPSA is that marketers know they're paying for something social and relationship-oriented. More importantly, marketers know that they're not specifically paying for exposure, traffic, conversions, or interactions."

This is a valid way to add soft metrics to your ROI grid, with the caveat that active participants at a social media site may not reflect the bulk of the visitor population. It's estimated that only one percent of community members who visit social media destinations take any action at all. The other ninety-nine percent will simply view content or comments. While not "active" they may be absorbing a brand-related message. Clearly they have less value to the marketer than an active participant.

What's It Worth to You? Calculating Cost Figures for Social Media

Agencies committed to selling "buzz" are doing their best to educate marketers about where social media can fit directly into the sales funnel.

"Right now, any pay-per-tweet model is likely to start as a pay-per impression. Because really, a tweet is just viewed. If we pay for a tweet, we're paying for eyeballs," explains Brian Carter, Director of Social Media at Myrtle Beach–based Fuel Interactive. In mid-2009, Carter helped launch TweetROI.com, a "pay-per-tweet" twitter marketing service that sees the evolution of web metrics into a discipline that looks at both direct sales results and other types of conversions at the same time.

"The next question is: are social media clicks worth as much as PCC [pay per click] clicks?" he says. "You might be tempted to assume they are less. But the fact is . . . there are many possible goals for tweeting, from PR and brand awareness at one end of the spectrum to direct marketing at the other. These not only have different metrics, but also get radically different results in terms of direct measurable ROI."

As discussed in Chapter 2, one approach to finding ROI, at least predictive ROI, for what you'd pay a professional tweeter is to consider the Customer Lifetime Value of any new customer brought in by a purposeful tweet. Customer Lifetime Values do vary by product, but you can probably get that information fairly easily. The typical percentages for lead generation for other forms of word-of-mouth outreach may also be known by your sales management team; it's worth asking as these can be plugged into the equation, or used as benchmarks. If you don't have a rough percentage, ballpark an estimate as a benchmark goal. This will give you some insight when you're purchasing ad space on a social media site, or dedicating marketing dollars to staff or an outside firm to run a social media campaign.

For more on this, we'd recommend Jim Sterne's book, aptly titled *Social Media Metrics* (John Wiley & Sons, 2010) to anyone wishing to learn more advanced methods in data collection and interpretation techniques.

The Convergence: Social Media and Search

The elusive goal of making word-of-mouth trackable to sales or conversions will be taking a big stride forward soon. As with all things metric, Google is behind the big push. What's coming may be shocking.

Perhaps the best reason to keep an eye on brand mentions in social media is that Facebook and Twitter are starting to get counted in Google, Yahoo!, and Microsoft searches, as of late 2009, although, a few protocols later, Facebook's current privacy settings do not allow a complete Google search. Astute minds in the industry point out that this will affect search results for your brand or product, and is bound to affect your budget for paid search. All the finely honed automated bidding systems are likely to be skewed with bloated additions of pages and pages of tweets that surface in the search process. If you thought "clutter" was the bane of TV and radio advertising, you ain't seen nothin' like the noise from a thousand chattering keyboards following Britney, Madonna, or the latest global weather disaster.

Google's own data (from Google Insights for Search and other reports) supports this trend: Social media searches rose 400 percent in 2009 (see Figure 3-5), and that figure may double in 2010, while other searches remained fairly flat.

"It's Google that's driving social media searches way, way up," says web analyst Marshall Sponder, whose popular blog on social media measurement (www.webmetricsguru.com) has been covering the topic for interested parties. "The inclusion of updates from Twitter and Facebook are the main drivers—but the overall direction is for a full integration between search engines and social media."

Ian Schafer, CEO of DeepFocus, has looked at the $750 million acquisition of the AdMob mobile advertising network by Google as the last piece of the puzzle—being able to acquire, potentially, the word-of-mouth digital trails on your mobile phone.

"With the acquisition of AdMob, Google now has access to usage

Figure 3-5 Social media rises 400 percent.

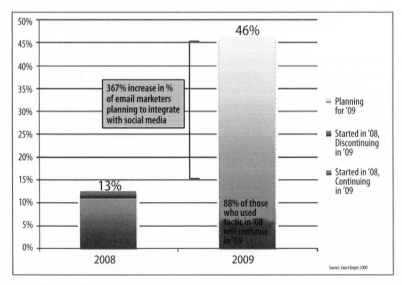

Source: ExactTarget, 2009

data of many of the popular mobile apps, especially the apps in the iTunes App Store. For iPhones." The move was nearly simultaneous with the launch of Android, Google's mobile phone platform. As Schafer points out: "If Google is taking on Apple for the mobile operating system market share, they just scored a huge competitive advantage. . . . Now, even if you don't own an Android phone, Google will be able to collect data."

The fight is definitely on. Apple more recently acquired Quattro Wireless, to parry Google's AdMob purchase, and shortly thereafter restricted AdMob and other competitors from collecting information key to the mobile ad market, such as the geographic location of users.

The gold mine for Google will be mobile display advertising that is geocentric and geo-targeted. Sponder notes with interest the creation of a bar-code reader-related ad platform that is in its baby stages as we write this. (For more, see *Special Section: Measuring with Marshall* at the end of Chapter 6). Another early example is a joint project of the geocentric social media site Foursquare (www.foursquare.com) with the Time Out magazine chain. Time Out publishes city guides for dining and entertainment (both print and online) and sells local as well as national ads. When Foursquare patrons use a mobile phone or PDA to geo-locate their friends for a night on the town, the tiny screens can serve up notices of drink specials, free pizza, or discount show tickets from the nearest advertising clients.

Foursquare was courted by (and turned down) a $100 million buyout from Yahoo! back when it only had about 150,000 users. Now with 2 million participants, and primarily young adults, it is still on the auction block, and should spawn leagues of competitors in mobile ad marketing. The relatively small populations of geocentric social media sites (among them Gowalla and Loopt) make them ripe for all sorts of experimentation in the near future.

And Keep an Eye On . . .

Both Twitter and Facebook developers continue to evolve into platforms suitable for branding initiatives that can be cross-referenced with actual sales data. The year 2008 saw the launch of Twitpay, a group of applications first trotted out to aid nonprofits. Naturally, this has a future as an e-commerce platform, a kind of PayPal for Twitter, so no one was surprised when Twitpay was acquired in 2010 by an investor group led by Ashish Bahl, the CEO of Acculynk, an online banking services company. Currently PayPal is used for many transactions in the Twitter universe and Twitpay is still being used only by charities, such as United Way and the Arthritis Foundation. The charities post (i.e., tweet) a request for donations. To make a payment, the donor merely reposts or retweets the message. This action authenticates the transfer of money, provided both donor and nonprofit have TwitPay accounts. The parent company takes 5 percent of the transaction, which can confirm in about 72 hours; this is a big improvement over mobile phone charity operations that often charge as much as 20 percent and take as long as 60 or 90 days to process a donation. The speed of the transaction makes Twitpay attractive to merchants who may wish to experiment with Twitter as a direct sales channel.

Facebook is also changing how merchant developers can capture and track commenters. Previously, third-party users of the site could only hold and share user data for twenty-four hours; at Facebook's F8 Developer Summit in April 2010, it was announced that third-party users could keep the user data forever. Further, this data could include not just what users posted on Facebook about a product or company, but their other connections—likes, dislikes, whom they fanned or followed, and even their posted city or hometown. How this shakes up among privacy advocates and the public at large is unknown, but the changes currently make it easier to identify and woo brand advocates, track leads over time, and more accurately measure Facebook comment effects on the bottom line.

To sum up: what seems immeasurable can at least be estimated for predictive purposes in ROI equations. Just decide ahead of time if the events you are counting are directly trackable to sales, or if you will use them as either proxy measures or for the purpose of comparing expenditures to reach the same population. Mapping both types of initiatives—branding as well as direct sales pitches—to your sales results will become easier as it goes along.

Mapping Marketing ROI to the Sales Funnel

WHETHER YOU ARE B-to-B, B-to-C, or a nonprofit, your marketing efforts can be viewed through a technique called the *sales funnel*. We recommend you try this, visually and organizationally, to help to fine-tune the ROI of all your marketing investments; it will provide a very clear picture of the value returned for specific segments of your marketing spend. Nearly all forms of marketing—even the elusive word of mouth—can be placed within a sales funnel.

Marketing, at its heart, is geared to *lead generation*. Lead generation spurs sales, and sales departments—whether they are down the hall or in a call center in another continent—have many tools at their disposal to track leads and determine sales performance for many types of leads. Your organization probably already has sales force automation tools in place, and if you're not familiar with these tools, you should consider sitting down with your sales department peers to see what they are using. Not that you may wish to use the same tools they are, but this can be a good start to creating your own sales funnel techniques for marketing.

The funnel-shaped (yes!) dashboard indicators now common to online marketing have been a wake-up call to all marketers. Figure 4-1 shows a simple dashboard from Unica.

Marketing's use of the typical sales funnel is a little different from sales' use. Sales force automation concentrates on finding customers: salespeople are given prospects to call, or they comb through prospects gathered from outreach (inbound calls or website registration) or paid leads (such as paid lists or paid referrals). Typical sales force tools are great for this, but they rarely include the information necessary to calculate ROI figures for what can be the largest expenditure in marketing—the cost of establishing and maintaining the brand.

Figure 4-1. Dashboard with a funnel function.

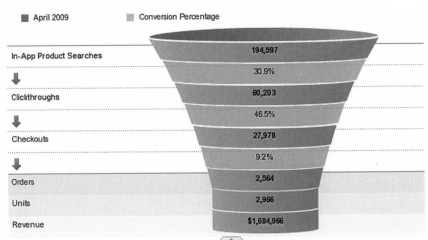

Marketing, however, is all about making it easy for customers to find *you*. Your branding metrics, fuzzy as they are, can be applied to a sales funnel. In fact, they have a place at the top of the sales funnel. It is not difficult to construct a pipeline with CRM tools that acknowledges branding messages. Reach, frequency, engagement, etc. can be noted as proxy measures. But you don't have to measure them strictly or accurately. It's enough to acknowledge they are there, and smart to include their costs. This can be an eye-opener.

Branding at the Top

As we've said, the typical sales force automation funnel has leads at the top. A marketing sales funnel adds an upper layer that represents your branding efforts and your branding expense.

A simple funnel would include *all* your branding expenses that relate directly to marketing—advertisements, local or national event sponsorships, social media campaigns, flyers with coupons, viral e-mail campaigns, etc. Figure 4-2 shows one way to visualize this kind of funnel.

Anne Giles Clelland of Handshake Media Inc. (www.handshake20.com) concocted this chart to help her marketing agency clients visualize the often amorphous effects of branding media, which can be key to introducing a new product or firm.

Aggregating the entire branding spend in your calculations does away with the headache of attribution for individual efforts. This can be helpful if online marketing is a single budget line item, as it is with many smaller organizations, or if branding is lumped with the public relations spend.

Says Clelland, "As a social media PR and advertising agency, we use social media on behalf of our clients and also with our own company. It's important to say at the outset that the use of social media

Figure 4-2. Social media and the sales funnel.

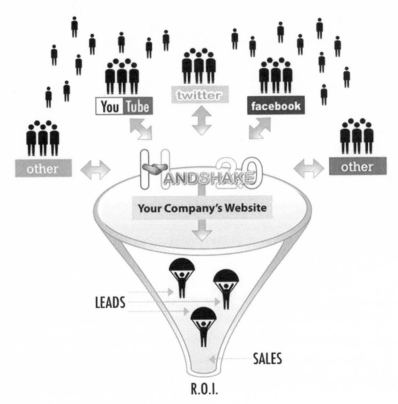

Credit: Kelsey Sarles for Handshake Media Inc.

and sales are not causal and conditional—i.e., if a company uses social media, then a new sale will result. The use of social media can bring potential clients and customers to the top of the sales funnel, and this begins the sales process."

The point of branding is to bring customers close enough to the funnel, pulling them in as they drift by from the universe. They may be drifting by as they walk through the parking lot of the strip mall where your store is located, or they may be surfing Twitter or an industry insider bulletin board on their office computers.

Says Clelland, "That potential customers come closer to the top of a company's sales funnel, because of the value of the information and conversation found in the company's use of social media, is a fine and reasonable expectation to have." However, she warns, "Expecting immediate use of social media to result in immediate sales will result in immediate disappointment."

The usual timeline for mapping a sales funnel is three months, and that's plenty of time to examine key touch points on the way to a sale. Esco Strong, senior group manager of the Atlas Institute, agrees that branding measures belong at the top of the funnel as the first set of touch points.

"It's a myopic view that disregards the points at the top of the funnel that brought the consumers down to the bottom." Mr. Strong added, "You make someone aware at the top of the funnel, target them with specific information in the middle, and drive them to buy with search at the end."

If you like, you can break down branding initiatives individually, creating a separate funnel for each one in order to track their respective abilities to generate sufficient leads. In this case, noting the costs of each measure at the top of the funnel can be worthwhile, though you should not expect to find true ROI numbers so far up the funnel. Looking realistically at branding at the top of the funnel means disregarding proxy measures such as "intent to purchase." It's better to concentrate on behaviors. And that's where the real funnel fun begins.

Building a Marketing Spend Funnel

This exercise takes the disciplines used in lead generation and lead reporting and applies it to your marketing outreach. The dollar figures involved are your *marketing expense* and your resulting *revenues*, if sales is the wanted conversion of the spend.

There are the steps involved in creating a useful marketing funnel program.

Step 1: Measure or quantify your marketing expense.

Step 2: Measure only actual leads.

Step 3: Qualify or identify the most promising leads and lead streams.

Step 4: Woo the qualified leads with additional outreach.

Step 5: Remove any remaining barriers to the conversion.

Step 6: Be sure to record the conversion *accurately*.

Step 1: **Measure Your Marketing Expense**   If you're brave, bite the bullet and include the entire marketing investment of an individual initiative, if not for an entire campaign that would include branding and direct marketing over several months. It's possible to slice and dice further, but try not to make yourself cross-eyed with figures.

The soft, airy top of your sales funnel—where people who use social media might come across your brand messages—is a good place to record soft metrics too. According to a study of 500 U.S. online marketers in April 2010, 60 percent of you are still using traffic—the click-through rate—as the main indicator of customer interest. CTRs have no direct relationship to sales (in fact the ratio these days is so bad it is inverse) according to an October 2009 Nielsen analysis of 200 online banner campaigns. In direct mail (or e-mail) the key soft metric is response rate (or open rate if that can be counted). In broadcast advertising, brand awareness studies such as recall or exposures are commonly counted. Those useless numbers for reach and frequency that you also use for print advertising finally have a home, up here in the stratospheric top of the funnel. In social media, gross numbers for mentions, forwards, and retweets that you're inputting into your ROI grid (see Chapter 2) can go at the top of the funnel for now.

Your marketing funnel will need a time frame—and that's different from a sales funnel too, especially if you're including branding as well as direct marketing expenses. Mapping your overall marketing spend to conversion results should be a leisurely process, as the path from exposure to conversion may take a very long time. Young-Bean Song, senior director at Microsoft Advertising Institute, shared an interesting study at a conference in January 2010, which looked at the activities of 200 advertisers on the web. The study average was that customers looked at between forty and fifty advertisements over roughly a month before they made an initial purchase.

For consumer appeals, one month to six months makes a good time frame. The more expensive or complex your product, the longer your time frame should be. Examples of products that benefit from long-range branding campaigns include wedding gowns, new cars, appliances or electronics equipment costing more than $500, financial products, and higher education. A month is usually sufficient to gauge results of campaigns for seasonal or impulse buys such as food products, packaged goods, small electronics, vacation packages, and entertainment products.

For business customers, branding campaigns need to be sustained and refreshed fairly constantly. From the first exposure to a new product or service, B-to-B sales completion may take six to twelve months, due to billing schedules, production schedules, returns, and client payment time lags.

Step 2: **Measure Only Actual Leads**   This is where measurement *really* begins—with actual leads being the hard top of the sales funnel.

Where do you start counting? An impression or a message is still out there floating in the stratosphere until your prospect starts heading down to earth and becomes an actual lead. This occurs when the prospect has *performed an action.*

Define what actions and behaviors typically lead to conversion. In the auto industry, the key action is taking a test drive; in other industries it could also be redeeming a coupon, asking for an RFP or requesting a price quote, or calling in for more information after exposure to an advertisement somewhere. For nonprofits, taking a flyer or visiting your information page isn't a trackable, lead-generating activity. However, tracking the visitors and seeing how many click on to the donation page prior to signing up for a newsletter might qualify as lead-generating, even if the prospect doesn't go all the way and make a donation at that time.

If your offering is information useful to a business, there's a big difference between interest and actions. Downloading your free whitepaper isn't a lead-generating activity, as you may never see that prospect again. Considering this an "action," a seriously overused tactic, is a mistake; it belongs with the branding strata of your funnel—the number of giveaways is a soft metric only. This is the online equivalent of handing out tote bags at the county fair with your business phone number on it; don't hold your breath waiting for a call.

If the prospect signs up for weekly newsletters, that's more promising, as this can create the opportunity for repeated brand and message exposures that may eventually hit the mark. Entering a contest or taking a free sample or free keychain or free download is not an actual lead, even if you have the prospect's contact information. In other words, opt-in lists are wonderful, but they're still only proxy measures that can't be counted on. The advantage to counting only specific actions is that it allows you, later on, to analyze cost-per-action on your marketing expenses to help improve your ROI.

Step 3: **Qualify or Identify the Most Promising Leads and Lead Streams**   Online, there are many simple tools that provide strategies to winnow leads from the fluff and chaff of traffic.

Yahoo!'s Conversion-Only Analytics package (free with Yahoo! ad services) tracks only conversion events, such as purchasing a product, or registering for a conference. This tracking is done on a confirmation page or a "thank you" page that appears after the transaction or action has been completed. This page has a special coding tag that can be linked to inbound traffic or ad click-throughs. The feature also allows you to count revenue attached to each kind of action. "Constant average value" is the formula used for sales if revenue is the same for each transaction (for example, a $1.99 download of a ringtone). "Dynamic value" is the formula used when revenue per transaction will vary (a customer purchases two blouses, two skirts, and a pair of shoes).

How can you apply conversion-only tracking to your real-world leads? Consider the "thank you." In retail it's often a coupon printed upon a store receipt, tempting the customer to return; the retailer can accurately track the rate of return for the coupon.

The updates in Google Analytics were a giant step in helping to qualify inbound web traffic as actual leads. For example, you can identify all visitors by profiling them according to up to twenty action goals. These goals include newsletter sign-up, a click-through to the "contact" page, catalog or information request, product information page views, time on site, pages per visit, product drop into shopping cart, and completion of transaction. What's more, you can now run custom reports that show only the activities of "unique" visitors not previously in your database.

If you don't think this is a big deal, a year ago Google only allowed up to four actions tabulated per visitor. This makes Google Analytics, a free program with its twenty categories, into a sales force automation engine for lead reporting.

Qualifying leads in the real world can be done on paper. Once you've collected prospect data (name, date, and what the prospect wanted), you may be able to do a spreadsheet that helps you rank your prospects, say on a 1 to 5 scale, and then group the prospects by customer type or product type. You can then hand this information to the sales department, electronically or in person.

Qualifying leads can also be done on the fly. Go into any major retail chain—from Victoria's Secret to Duane Reade—and one of the first things a salesperson will ask is if you are a member of their loyalty card program. This helps separate new customers from existing customers; at the checkout, matching the purchase with the customer's status or profile specifics helps generate subsequent offers sent by mail or e-mail. Smaller operations can train their sale staffs to ask, "Have you visited our store before?" to sharpen opportunities for upsell and cross-sell.

Attribution: Always a Question

To accurately identify leads through the conversion funnel, all marketing messages should provide an action opportunity. Marketers accustomed to legacy forms of branding, such as sponsorships or "informational" media, may well balk at turning this type of prancing pony into a performance-based workhorse. Yet best practices would argue that no organizational communication should be without some call to action. If you're passing out plastic tote bags at the county fair, you make sure your 800 phone number is on them. It's rare to see a sponsored video these days without at least a website URL. But both messages are passive and would be improved by providing an opportunity for interaction. The tote bag could say, "Call for a free estimate" and the TV program might switch from a URL to a texting site, inviting the viewer to comment on the show. Cable reality shows such as *American Idol, Top Chef,* and *Project Runway* popularized the text-as-you-watch call to action, now being adapted by news programs.

Given the increasing complexity of the digital conversion funnel, one pitfall to avoid is attributing too much weight to the last interaction. Online, this is often the "last click." Offline, this is often the customer's approach to the sales counter or the phone call placing the order. Savvy marketers seek to discover the customer's path prior to the order. Granted, if all you're doing is e-commerce, this is much easier to achieve.

A 2009 study by Microsoft Advertising for Alltel, a wireless phone service company, looked at all digital touch points available in a consumer's online history. Consumers (potential purchasers) collected from computer users who clicked onto a search advertisement were segmented into two groups. The first, "search clickers," were computer users who clicked on an Alltel-sponsored search term but their histories revealed no exposure to branded advertising. A second group, "search and display," clicked on a sponsored search term but their online histories showed they had been exposed to at least one Alltel branding banner on a website.

The study used as a reference, or benchmark, a previous study that showed computer users exposed to both a branding ad and a search ad were 22 percent more likely to convert (i.e., purchase) than those who arrived on the site through search exclusively. The newer Alltel study found that computer users exposed to both branding and search were in fact 56 percent more likely to convert than those who clicked on a search term while searching online for a phone service provider.

The results, which represented 96 percent of the total sales associated with the online initiatives, were applied to ROI comparison measures that depreciated the amount of sales credited to the search channel by 60 percent. Of seven display ad sites, it was found that the four largest display sites might rightly claim 33 percent of the conversions within their ad-spend ROI. The statistics themselves were recorded by a third-party ad server (Ingenuity Media). This has profound implications to marketers who spend the bulk of their dollars on search. The take-away is that display can't be ignored, and where eyeballs or cookies can be tracked, attributing conversions may indeed be higher up (earlier) than the last interaction. That's another reason why branding needs to be a part of the conversion funnel, above first actions.

Online or offline, the simpler solution for the metrics-challenged is to create direct-response opportunities and build them into all your marketing messages, even within social media. It's a solution that works even for nonprofits, and even if your mission is not to sell goods, but ideas for living.

A 140-character tweet is long enough to announce a special offer, with a link to a specific landing page set up by the organization. The offer can be a coupon code, or a free video, or white paper. The landing page (an appended site or inside page) can include a registration hoop—a few fields to capture e-mail and name—to allow for tracking through a CRM system.

The poster child for this is Dell, which has claimed it has made over $1 million in sales directly attributed to Twitter alerts.

Consumers can sign up to follow Dell's Twitter alerts, generally messages about products at special discounts at its online outlet, which sells refurbished, returned, and discontinued models.

The American Red Cross also uses Twitter, to rally its volunteers for both disaster work and fundraising. Red Cross has over 14,000 active followers; Dell has more than 1,500,000 at last count.

Marketing consultant Patrick McGraw (www.patmcgrawmarketing.com) notes that organizations playing to a younger audience can use Twitter alerts successfully, and has used similar techniques for his corporate and university clients. Responses to B-to-B free offers, such as offering a download of a white paper on a relevant topic, can move ahead from mere branding to a true lead if you follow up at your end by providing a destination page that collects contact information that can be followed up, such as an email address or Twitter screen name.

Says McGraw:

> Any time you extend an offer, do it in a way that allows you to track performance. I use bit.ly [www.bit.ly.com] to help track performance—that little darling of a service tells me how many clicked on the link, where they are located (what country), and what days the link was sent out and clicked.
>
> Unique landing pages are key—and personalization helps too! The friendlier you are, the more likely you will get a little more information on the buyer so you can score, prioritize, and determine whether or not the buyer is qualified, sales-ready, or in need of further nurturing.

But don't just twitter or analyze the talk streams—turn responses to any free offer into actual leads with a follow-up, perhaps a week later. If you're B-to-B, you might ask if they found the downloaded white paper of value, and inquire if they have done business with your company before. If they have, ask for information that links their Twitter screen name with an existing account. If the Twitter offer resulted in a purchase, then you have billing data that includes a Twitter screen name that can be matched up to an existing account, or to a newly created account. Either way, you've obtained measurable data that can be linked to sales data in your ROI calculations.

TWEET POWER

When the message is compelling, the results of a text campaign can be staggering, as was illustrated by the International Red Cross Haitian relief campaign, which raised $2 million in donations over a two-day period following Haiti's devastating 2009 earthquake. The mechanism was deceptively simple: text the word "Haiti" to a number and $10 would be donated to the Red Cross, added on to the user's next monthly phone bill. Beneath the awesomeness of this public effort—more than $7 million in donations was raised the first week—lies a system that could readily be adapted for impulse purchasing at a concert, sporting event, or while watching a film or TV program.

Step 4: **Woo the Most Qualified Leads**   Once you have identified the prospect as a new or potential customer, initiate real conversations. By phone, by e-mail, or in person, marketing to this group takes a different tack. This is not the group to offer contests or giveaways or samples unless you have a new product line you are introducing. It's a waste to give free stuff to existing customers, except as a thank you that can also be tracked to subsequent conversion activity.

This is where to get creative. Goosing the good prospect toward the sale is the place for e-mail-only or newsletter-only discounts (generated through trackable coupon codes) or special invitation only in-store events. Don't inundate the prospect—twice or at most three times a month is fine for e-mails or social media messaging. And you can experiment and A/B test the messages to see which pull in conversions best. Keep time frames short for these special offers—price-based promotions can be expensive and most burn out on the third day. And remember to add the cost of these promotions to your ROI.

The 80/20 rule applies of course; if you've accurately qualified your leads by a specific action or conversion, the lower levels of your sales funnel are now getting pretty skinny. Some actions you might like to take are allowing current or prospective customers to help customize or suggest new products. This is routinely done by software and hardware manufacturers in the business-to-business arena and helps create a dialogue that builds brand familiarity. Allowing potential customers to "vote" on a new cupcake flavor or survey them for the best location for a branch office are some other examples. When you ask customers for feedback, extra costs are minimal and the engagement level improves.

Don't let your leads sit. The maximum response time to a phone or e-mail query should be twenty-four hours or less, yet this is hardly the case even with many Fortune 500 companies. It is one area the smaller organization can get a leading edge. If your company doesn't have CRM or sales force automation tools that help you direct leads to the proper department or division, you may wish to develop a system in-house with your office staff, sales staff, and public relations team to assign responsibilities to follow up with potential customers, so that they can be directed in a timely manner to sales personnel or customer service. Your switchboard or call center should be informed of the additional marketing outreach you are using specifically for your most promising leads. Make sure they are trackable by a tag of some kind. The most common types of tagging for business-to-business lead tracking are dedicated toll-free or switchboard numbers for specific marketing channels or mailers, or CRM-based systems that assign certain dedicated toll-free numbers based on the area code of the caller.

Step 5: **Remove Any Remaining Barriers to the Sale**   If that last paragraph seemed odd to you, it may be because many marketing managers remain at arm's length—if not a continent's length—from the actual sales process. That bottleneck at the bottom of your sales funnel may be your organization's call center. If they don't know about a special promotion, they may lose the sale (or whatever conversion is required) anticipated by the additional marketing push to top prospects. Thinking through the process, and then enlisting the help of your associates in sales, customer service, or top management *prior* to the additional marketing is recommended. Expect that some barriers can only be discovered in the aftermath and after a full funnel view and review.

Still, you can anticipate probable barriers to a sale and use them in the additional messaging to your top prospects. If your organization beats the competition by features or price, put together a comparison chart as part of your marketing collateral. If competitors are beating you on price, play up customer service and include guarantees. If price is a stumbling block entirely, offer "special financing information for new customers only," which can simply be a clearer, plainer-language rundown of financing options than appear in the tiny print on a catalog or brochure. And don't forget to A/B test each iteration to find the one that works best.

Step 6: **Be Sure to Record the Conversion *Accurately*** If your desired conversion is an actual sale, get the revenue numbers for your campaign's time frame from your sales department or head office. Other types of conversions, such as sign-ups or RFP requests, can be hand-entered in a spreadsheet that can be turned into a funnel graph.

You may have to build in a time lag specific to your organization's sales process or adjust or extend your time frame to capture all conversions that should be credited. At minimum, look at numbers with a thirty-day time lag when examining a conversion funnel that includes a branding campaign. As with the ROI grid discussed in Chapter 2, you'll want to decide ahead of time when and how you will recount returns or preorders that won't be billed for a month or more.

Analyzing Funnel Data for ROI

To get data into a visual funnel, use a dashboard program or make your own from the many templates available to those who have access to IT talent in-house. One example to look at is FunnelCake, which was created by ace programmer Joshua Krall for TransFS.com, a comparison-shopping website for credit card processing.

TransFS lets businesses find a better deal on credit card processing fees, when they use an auction service and comparison engine on the TransFS site. (The process is similar to mortgage comparison services such as Lending Tree.) The company advertises over the web and tracks traffic. However, users who visit the site and try the service must input information and go through multiple steps to complete an auction. FunnelCake was developed as a method for visualizing which parts of the conversion funnel could be improved to raise the overall conversion rate. One thing we like about this example is that the first hard measurement is not website traffic, but visits to a specific page where a customer action first occurs.

The program is available as freeware; Krall's development blog and the company's own business blog include this among many thoughtful discussions on methods small businesses can use to measure marketing performance. See more at: http://transfs.com/devblog/2009/03/26/sales-funnel-visualization-and-tracking-with-funnelcake/

If your goal is specifically revenue, you can easily work your way back up the funnel to measure the comparative effectiveness of your marketing investments. For example, you can determine your cost-per-

Figure 4-3. The conversion funnel of an auction marketplace.

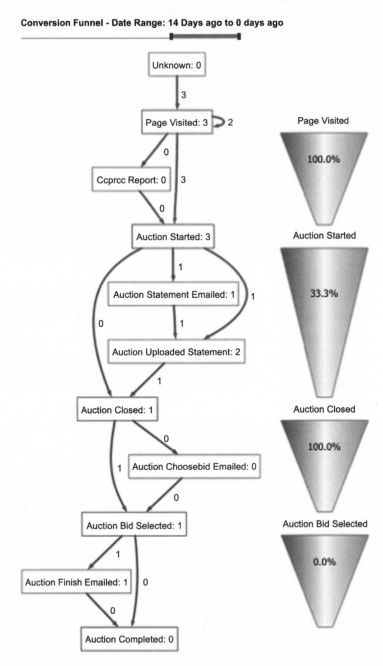

lead as a cost-per-action measurement. You will also get a good estimate, useful for benchmarking, that tells you how many leads you need to acquire in order to complete one conversion or sale. In other words, if you find on average that you need 200 qualified leads to make one $50 sale, then your cost per lead is 25 cents.

Using Dashboards

Dashboards are popular for online marketing, and most everyone wants some now. Most of the marketing suites used for ad tracking, including free services such as Google Analytics or Yahoo! Web Analytics, offer even the smallest company the convenience of real-time monitoring that links conversions to campaigns. And there are many marketing firms and open-source heroes who supply dashboard templates for offline marketing uses.

The main problem with dashboarding is that there are so many things you could count, and a lot of things that are easy to count but not useful for ROI calculations, such as click-through rates. Dashboard design should be built around your specific key performance indicators, otherwise known as KPI. Another problem with off-the-shelf dashboards is that standard KPIs may not reflect the things you need to measure the most.

To build a dashboard, here are some considerations to think about first:

1. *Make sure your KPIs reflect your marketing goals.* Is your performance success measured by sales revenue, or units sold? Or is it measured by outreach and engagement? A KPI for engagement might be the percentage of customers who return, or the number who sign up

for a weekly newsletter, or the percentage who refer your business or service to other parties.

For a startup business, traffic may be a good indicator and is worth including. A mature business whose goal is growth might be more focused on the number of "new" or "unique" customers obtained since the last quarter year.

Keep the number of elements small. Five KPIs per dashboard is just about all the executive mind can handle. If you want more than that, both custom and off-the-shelf dashboards can be set up as modular, with an "executive summary" that shows the main trends.

Your goals will also need a time frame. Between one month and three months is a good range if you're trying to tie goals to specific campaigns; one year or one week may be just right for certain marketing events, such as a year-long anniversary promotion that gets a lot of press, or a one-week sales drive.

A good many dashboards allow you to figure in the time lag between campaign launch and absorption by the marketplace. This is important, as it can take on average thirty days for an online branding campaign to begin to impact sales, according to studies by Microsoft's Atlas Institute.

2. *Make sure your KPIs are quantifiable.* This is easy online—not so easy offline. You can count website traffic easily but in-store traffic may need a human to count. You may have noticed museum attendants deploying a hand-clicker device to track traffic into an exhibit, and store personnel can use them at the front door or in specific departments or counters to give you a rough estimate where customers are going. (If you're not sure what we mean, type "hand clicker" into ebay.com or a search engine.)

Know what you are measuring in terms of revenue reporting as well. Are you measuring gross sales, or do the numbers reflect returns?

If so, are returns calculated into sales for the previous month, or the month where they occur?

3. *Make your KPIs known to the organization, and accessible.* Your dashboard is going to have some lovely charts and graphs. Share them. Post them in the break room. Some managers may wince at making current numbers accessible to staff or to media partners, but this can be a powerful tool to encourage ROI thinking within your sphere of office influence. If others can see your data, they may be able to spot trends or anomalies that your busy self may miss.

Of course, to do this your dashboard is going to have to be quite simple so everyone from the receptionist fielding complaint calls to the mail clerk sending out billing notices can understand it, and see where progress is or is not being made.

If this scares you, then decide firsthand who beside yourself should be viewing the dashboard. If this includes C-level executives, ask them what numbers they would like to see, either in real time, or as part of an executive summary.

Simple Dashboards

You can build a dashboard using Excel either by cutting-and-pasting data into cells before running formulas through the program, or you can import data from an existing external database. SharePoint, another Microsoft app, is also used. There are a number of products that can convert the data into attractive bar charts or pie graphs, such as Anychart, which uses Flash (www.anychart.com).

Do-it-yourselfers might want to check out the Dashboard Spy blog, which offers hundreds of templates as well as product reviews (www.dashboardspy.com).

Most off-the-shelf dashboards can be customized, and most companies that sell them allow free trials and offer demos and examples on their websites. A few to consider:

Centerview: www.corda.com/centerview

Cognos 8 and Cognos Advisor: http://www-01.ibm.com/software/data/cognos/products/cognos-expres s/advisor/

Xcelsius, Flynetviewer: www.flynetviewer.com

Via, Strada, and custom dashboards: www.truviso.com

Your dashboard should run as a pilot program for the first three to six months before you make the data available to others in your organization. The pilot should also be a small-scale test. Pick a single product or product category, or a region, and plot the numbers for a while. Along the way, you may want to tweak how you measure your KPIs and how data is included into the system.

More Fun with Dashboards

With the rise of social media, agencies have been pushing methods to gauge, in real time, how a company or product is faring among the buzz. So now we get "reputation monitoring" dashboards. Marty Weintraub of AimClear recently blogged how to rig one up using Google Alerts and a little-known search utility, Boardreader (www .boardreader.com), to find mentions of product, brand, company personnel, and "intent phrases" such as "buy," "hate," "love," etc.

Marshall Sponder (www.socialmediaguru.com) regularly reports on social media marketing dashboarding techniques. See the special section "Measuring with Marshall" in Chapter 6 for a sample.

CASE STUDY #3

Nike Sees a Jump with Viral Video

Visible Measures, a Boston-based Web Video measurement firm, has made available a Viral Video case study of a Nike sneaker campaign that revolved around a web video featuring professional basketball player Kobe Bryant. We think this is an excellent illustration of the strengths and weaknesses of measuring peer-to-peer and social media branding of a consumer product. It also shows the value of soft metrics and proxy measures as useful pointers to ROI calculations.

In support of their Hyperdunk basketball shoe, Nike launched a viral video featuring Bryant recklessly leaping over a speeding Aston Martin. The video's low-end production quality makes the clip appear to be user-generated. As Visible Measures' analysis uncovered, this video was spread far and wide as the online viewing audience tried to figure out if one of the world's biggest sports stars would actually attempt such a stunt. Watch the YouTube clip below, then read on to see just how effectively this campaign drove audience reach: http://www.youtube.com/watch?v = cPNrxl—CLY.

The Viral Reach Database system captured well over 250 unique placements for the Kobe video. The brand appeared to be responsible for posting just over a dozen of the placements, so the remaining 250+ placements were *community-driven*. Of these, 60 percent were copies of the original video and 40 percent were derivative videos, ranging from reenactments of the stunt, to parodies of the clip, to a truth squad of viewers determined to reveal the video as a fake. The large number of viral placements reflects the clip's overall audience appeal.

The original and viral placements of the Hyperdunk Campaign accumulated more than 16 million views in aggregate. The original Kobe clips posted by Nike generated less than 40 percent of the overall reach. The viral placements increased the campaign reach by over 200 percent.

All told, the Nike Hyperdunk viral video campaign attracted over 35,000 comments. Based on a term frequency analysis, the audience reacted strongly to the campaign. Many of the comments collected reflect admiration ("best," "must-see") and skepticism ("fake," "real," "stunt").

The engagement curve for the Hyperdunk video demonstrates a number of viral phenomena. First, the clip's initial attention score indicates considerable audience abandonment during the clip's opening. However, as Kobe takes flight, the engagement curve spikes significantly, indicating substantial rewind behavior as viewers watch the stunt again (most likely to try to see if it was real or not). Finally, the downward slope at the end of the clip indicates moderate concluding abandonment as users realize the fun is over and click away from the video.

By combining their True Reach analysis with the audience interaction data from the Engagement Curve (see the final figure below), Visible Measures estimated the campaign's aggregate viewing time, which in this case represents total brand exposure. This campaign featured a highly compelling video that inspired massive viral activity. As a result, the estimated engaged reach of this campaign was a whopping 375,000 hours of total viewing time. For perspective, the original 54-second clip above drove well over 40 viewing *years* in aggregate! Perhaps this proves that one recipe for viral video success involves combining a major sports celebrity with an exotic car and an apparent near-death experience.

Visible Measures' Seraj Bharwani was interviewed by Noah Mallin in Reprice Medi's Search Views blog (http://www.searchviews.com/index.php/archives/2009/05/social-med a-5-question s-with-seraj-bharwani-of-visible-measures.php) in May 2009. In the interview, Seraj elaborated on Nike's pair of wildly successful viral video campaigns, the one with Kobe Bryant jumping over a speeding Aston Martin, and another with Ronaldinho volleying a soccer ball off the goal post from midfield. The original ads can be seen at the following URLs: Kobe Bryant at http://www.youtube.com/watch?v = 7h WJkdUMiMw and Ronaldinho at http://www.youtube.com/watch?v = i_ JS1YG8H2c.

Bharwani suggests that successful viral video campaigns share several common attributes:

> They challenge audience expectations. Entertainment value trumps all else. The video must capture audience imagination and keep them at the edge of their seats for what happens next. Videos that really take off in views have an *unbelievable* aspect to them. They engender audience curiosity as to whether a clip represents reality or just plain illusion—can someone actually jump over a speeding car or volley a soccer ball off a goalpost from 50 feet away? This creates the allure of mystery and discovery, attracting a broader community to investigate and comment on the true nature of the video. This also plays into the unbelievable nature of successful videos.
>
> They leave room for community participation. Intrigue over a video being real or not leaves room for audience speculation and involvement. Campaigns with audience opinions on either side of the camp generate buzz and draw more people into the dialog.
>
> The last piece of the viral puzzle is the celebrity factor. Campaigns can garner significant attention by involving a celebrity in a way that challenges audience expectations.

Figure 4-4 contains the graphs showing the soft metrics of the campaign.

While we can't speculate on the ROI of the Nike campaign spend, there are a few takeaways that the average marketing executive can relate to.

The first is that Nike paid for the production of the video, and spent some resources on its initial distribution on the web, through YouTube and through seeding. While the value of the multiplied placements distributed virally can't be determined, any more than true word of mouth can, it was possible to track the video's viral path. Exposures to the video ("impressions" if you like)

Figure 4-4. Nike soft metrics data.

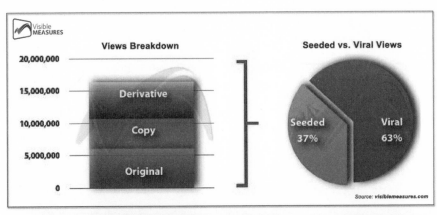

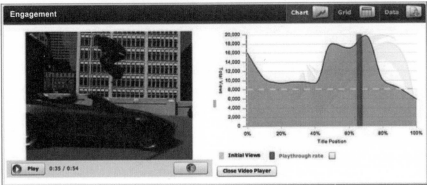

Source: visiblemeasures.com

could also be counted and in this case were comparable to exposure to a broadcast television campaign (as they may have been). The marketing investment of dollars spent would have been easy to identify, and gross sales of the shoe during the period the video was popular could serve as the net revenue part of the equation.

CHAPTER 5

Best Practices

Budgeting and Projecting Marketing ROI

IN TRADITIONAL BUSINESS FINANCE, it's not uncommon for a company to specify the ROI performance it expects for all new products, as well for product lines, geographic territories, and often, for each and every segment of the enterprise. In this view, all product lines are responsible for a rational return in exchange for the company's investment in them. Even more so, each department—and that includes support, marketing, public relations, and the executive suite—are called upon to recognize the dollar figure of the company's investment in them, and pursue the strategies to improve their own ROI.

If you're working in a recently downsized corporation, government bureau, or nonprofit organization, you've no doubt seen how this works when times are bad. The usual method is to fire busloads of staff, discontinue product, close stores, reduce hours, and cut back on nonessentials until the budget is cut down to the bone.

All of this, while whittling expenses, may temporarily affect bottom lines but does little to enhance the return on the ongoing investment in remaining staff, machinery, raw materials, and marketing support.

For the marketing department, the best defense is to finely slice and dice its ROI. Give each marketing initiative its own ROI goal, using standard performance metrics, and you will go a long way toward discovering where your now limited budget will do the most good to achieve the overall goals of your organization.

It can be helpful to think of each initiative as responsible for its own ROI, as if it were a "profit center" or strategic business unit. This is especially helpful if your organization uses online marketing, where resources and costs will vary greatly depending on which of the many channels available you look at. After all, it costs a certain sum, in terms of staff time if nothing else, to pursue a relationship with an influential blogger in your marketplace. It costs more to maintain a robust paid-search program through Google, Yahoo!, or Bing. Both these newer initiatives might be funded with dollars pared off from the print/TV/radio/tradeshow marketing budget, which may still take up the larger share of the marketing budget as a whole.

Apples and Cows

Giving each initiative its own ROI prevents apples-to-apples comparisons of funding versus revenue for channels that could be anything from a television ad purchase to a freelance blogger. This is necessary because the variance is more like apples to oranges to grapes to mangosteens, mangosteens being perhaps that very next next *next* Internet marketing channel to emerge beyond the point of time this book is printed.

Creating ROI for each initiative, and in fact for each individual campaign, provides the most useful strategic data and answers the questions the C-level is asking: which of our marketing efforts are resulting in acceptable revenue flow to the company, and which ones are not?

This is where the cows come home—that is, the sacred cows. These are the programs that have been stuck in your marketing budget since year one. To name a few:

▶ Print advertising in a particular trade or consumer magazine.

▶ Sports or charity event sponsorship in community or region.

▶ Printed sales kits, mail order catalogs, or direct-mail appeals.

For some B-to-B companies, it is the massive cost of an annual trade show booth. Once these face-to-face events were critical, as sales staff would literally write up orders on the show floor. The sales orders were binding documents, thus *net revenues* could be projected, tracked, and directly attributed to the venue of the show. The *net revenues* could be directly fed into ROI calculations that also tracked the *marketing investment* of the trade show, which included the booth, staff time, travel and entertainment expenses, and marketing collateral or samples specifically used at the event. When economies and industries downsize, no one goes to trade shows—both buyers and sellers stay away. Orders are pursued by telephone or e-mail, and the face-to-face meeting can be a less expensive conference call or videoconference, so no one has to travel. While we still see business media headlines when major corporations pull out of an industry trade show, the knowledge that even the biggest players in your vertical market are rethinking these legacy investments should make you unafraid to do the same.

In fact, the press show is stealthily replacing the trade show as the platform for new-product launches. Press are invited as are key customers, but the hall is likely to be rented for a day. Products on tables replace expensive booth exhibits, and the dog-and-pony show may simply be a PowerPoint presentation and a chat from the CEO and/or a celebrity spokesperson. Others may be invited to view a live webcast; the "press kit" is likely to be a small postcard with a link to a website's press pages.

Now, certain of the legacy items in the list above may be there for other reasons. For example, the CEO is personally committed to the charity that is sponsored, or the stockholder relations department worries that not taking a booth might be seen as a signal of company woes and drive down the stock price.

Still, if you, as the marketing manager, have that sinking feeling that you're not really getting a good return of revenues from an investment in a legacy marketing vehicle, doing the ROI calculation for it can help you decide to keep it, lose it, or modify the budget allotted to it, based on hard facts, not emotion. A graphic such as a pie chart or sales funnel may help others in your organization understand what you are saying (see Chapter 4, "Building a Marketing Spend Funnel," for how to make one).

One practical result may be a decision to take all or some of these legacies out of the marketing budget entirely, if there is a separate departmental budget for public relations or investor relations. This is a brave step and it is often not within marketing's power to make this change. More typically, you'll still have to keep the legacy within your marketing budget, but you and all others in the organization will recognize it as a branding expense that is not subject to ROI.

Budgeting and Planning Online Campaigns with ROI

For online marketing, the breakdown of what to count falls into three baskets that reflect the traditional formulas: that is, *operational*, *performance*, and *predictive*. Let's view all these through the eyeglass of web analytics, so we can see the whole picture of how new, cross-channel marketing techniques can enhance the development of true ROI reporting to the C-suite.

In online marketing, the most common operational formulas are derived from your website's server report, generally known as the "site report." Figure 5-1 shows a typical site report. There's a lot of stuff on there—visitors, unique visitors, page views, time spent on site, resulting in an overall measurement of *traffic*.

As a marketing manager, you don't have time to view it all. So what's most important?

Figure 5-1. Typical site report summary, for a holiday shopping period in 2009.

Website Traffic Report (11/25/2009–11/30/2009)	
Total page requests:	376,654
Total consumer sessions:	33,512
Total consumer referrals:	25,645
Average daily page requests:	62,776
Average daily consumer sessions:	5,585
Average daily consumer referrals:	4,274
Average consumer page visits:	11
Average consumer session length:	12:05

A report like this can be deeply mined; for example, it's not only possible to see which referring URLs generate the best traffic into the company's website, it's also possible to see which external URLs are receiving the most traffic when customers leave the website.

For at least one web entrepreneur, the exit data is as interesting as the landing page reports. "I want to know where the customer is going when they leave my pages," he says. "Is she going straight to her Face-book page to make a comment about her shopping experience? Is she going to a competitor's site to comparison-shop on price?"

Analysis of activity with the pages of a website as described in a site report adds some clues to the sales funnel. It should be easy to see which pages prompt the most desired actions (site registration, free trial download, account setup or purchase, etc.) and which product lines or information pages are visited less often. Duration (time spent on each page visited) and abandonment (last page visited before leaving the site) should be examined with web design in mind, to tweak errors and optimize the customer experience.

E-commerce functions that are viewable within a site report are exportable to ROI grids. The most important of these is "shopping cart abandon" rates, as these may reveal a significant blockage at the narrowest part of the online sales funnel.

Over the years, online retailers have seen their fill of site reports and many of their innovations are workarounds for common issues. Amazon.com and bn.com actually don't permit shopping carts to be abandoned; they merely store your abandoned selections as your "wish list" to be retrieved next time you visit the site.

A second common operational formula is used to determine the success rates of paid search and paid advertising related to search. Note, please, that we said "success rate." Not ROI. All those lovely columns, figures, percentages etc. do indeed refer to actual dollars and cents (and for most enterprises it's mostly cents, or fragmented parts of a U.S. penny). They only tell you where your money went, in paid search or banner ad CPMs. They do not tell you the return on your investment in search or banner dollars; they do not tell you the ROI.

The range of Google products makes a good example—Adwords, AdSense, and the newer tools available through their purchase of the ad platforms of Doubleclick and, more recently, AdMob. The free web analytics tools that come with these products often give novice marketers the illusion that they're producing reports that reflect actual return on investment (see figure 5-1). But while they do translate into dollars paid out, they can only "return" statistics to help you examine and optimize your search costs to find the best performing keywords. Only the full cost of your search program, which may be a budgeted monthly expense, belongs in your calculations for ROI.

Figure 5-2. Sample Google Analytics page.

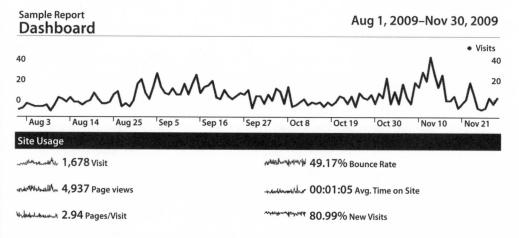

We have included a rundown of the most popular products for cross-channel analytics on the website associated with this book (http://www.marketingbythenumbers.com); however, we'd prefer not to endorse any single one, nor suggest you stick only to free services available. The website Top Ten Reviews (toptenreviews.com) does an annual rundown of software and you'll find their 2010 comparative survey of Web Analytics Tools here: http://web-analytics-review.top-tenreviews.com/index.html.

Comparing New Channels to Old

Is it fair to compare new channels to the old ones? This question is a serious one for advertisers who have relied on TV, radio, and print in the past. Today you are impelled to consider as separate channels online video, streaming podcasts, and of course the online versions of print publications. Repurposing designs and copy can be a cost saver, but is the cost of the online media buy an add-on, a bargain, or a waste of money?

Let's look at branding campaigns, for example, and some take-aways from a long-range study created by Beth Uyenco, Global Research Director for Microsoft Corporation, and David Kaplan, SVP of Research and Product Development for Nielsen. Their findings, presented at the 2010 annual meeting of the Advertising Research Foundation, were based on an exhaustive two-year study of TV and web video data that ran from November 2007 to May 2009. Their report gives the lie to any marketer who still thinks "there isn't enough data yet" to compare platforms. The study took place during a recessionary period in the Unites States that affected both advertiser and consumer budgets, as well as through eighteen months of seasonal buying.

Noting that online video ad spending increased 41 percent in 2009 (based on their own surveys) and that 72 percent of all Internet users do view video (borne out by several sources), Uyenco and Kaplan came to the conclusion that "online video outpaces TV when measured by the dollars marketers spend, relative to the amount of time individuals spend viewing video." In other words, it's a better buy.

But not a common buy. Which suggests opportunity for marketers while prices are low. What has held back many top brands, they said, is "the inability of the biggest TV advertisers to make a direct comparison between the effectiveness of TV and the effectiveness of an equivalent online buy."

Gross rating points (GRPs) are not the answer. "Can we use GRPs or impressions for evaluating both platforms? The answer is no," they said. However, soft metrics such as "general recall" could be, and were, used to measure the effectiveness of online video versus TV.

Here's how the study worked: the branding measurement was based on panels: along with panels of regular TV viewers, online TV viewers used a tagging device, IAG OpenTag. In this case panelists would go to a TV viewing website, view premium programming (one participant was Disney), and then would be directed to the polling website, RewardTV.com, where they were invited to take an optional survey. The individuals selected were only exposed to one platform, either regular TV or online. Another group of participants were exposed to both platforms.

Key metrics for the Nielsen IAG study were all soft:

1. *General recall:* Did those exposed to the ad remember the overall creative concept?
2. *Brand recall:* Did those exposed to the ad remember the brand the day after exposure?

3. *Message recall:* Did they remember the primary message the day after exposure?
4. *Likability:* Did those who remembered the brand the day after exposure report to like the ad "a lot" or "somewhat"?

In other words, a classic recall study (see Figure 5-3 below). Yet this survey covered 238 brands and 412 products. There were 951 individual ads ("ad executions") involved. About 14,000 participants completed the survey, and of those, about 7,500 were surveyed the day after.

But enough with the suspense. Let's look at their big takeaways:

Figure 5-3. Brand recall survey sample.

Ad Surveys for Premium Online Video and Linear TV Are Identical Allowing Direct Comparison of Platforms	

General Recall	• In an advertisement during this show, what happened that caused people to clap and cheer as a silver car sped along a desert highway?
	  – Grooves in asphalt sounded out a musical composition when driven over
	  – Nails in the ground held balloons that inflated when they were passed
	  – Miniature cones on short medians fell in a domino effect when clipped
	  – Colored lights on fence poles made a light show signaling traffic was clear

Brand Recall	• What was this advertisement for?
	  – Honda Civic
	  – Nissan Sentra
	  – Ford Focus
	  – Toyota Corolla

Message Recall	• According to this advertisement, why should you purchase a Honda Civic?
	  – Gets great gas mileage
	  – Seats five comfortably
	  – Has a powerful engine

Likability	• How much did you like this advertisement?
	  – I liked it a lot
	  – I liked it somewhat
	  – I am neutral about this advertisement
	  – I disliked it somewhat
	  – I disliked it a lot

Note: Responses randomized for General, Brand and Message Recall questions.

ARF **ADVERTISING RESEARCH** FOUNDATION

1. *Web video vs. regular TV*: Online video performed better than TV "across every brand metric and for every vertical." Online brand recall percentages online were 50 percent, compared to TV's 28 percent. The branding measurements were even more skewed when looking at younger viewers (age 13 and up).

2. *Web video and TV together*: Campaigns combining online video and TV ads improved recall and "likeability" by significant percentages for all verticals.

The study also looked to find which formats of online video advertising seemed to work best. The results of this study propose that video ads inserted (i.e., "in-stream") in short-form content generate better brand and message recall, and had better likeability. We think this is very understandable: viewers intent on viewing long-form programs on the web, such as entire TV sitcoms or entire films, want an immersible experience and find inserted ads an annoying distraction.

And you'll be glad to know the study found that repurposed TV ads were at least as effective as original online video advertisements, which means you can get more use out of that ad production spend.

Uyenco and Kaplan said strongly that GRPs and impressions can't be used to compare online video viewing to live or even time-shifted (VCR, DVR) viewing. But soft metrics such as recall can still serve as useful proxy measures, if you've got the budget for panels and customer surveys. We'd like to see similar testing among live radio and podcasts, and among print versus online versions of the same content in, say, a trade magazine. Until we do, there is one more takeaway from this study.

First, the question: why is online video viewing of an advertisement preferable to regular TV, if ad and message recall is an important soft metric for you? The answer is *engagement*. The online TV viewer has a far more intimate experience with online video—instead of a TV across the room, the computer screen is at arm's length—or less, if you're viewing video on a cell phone. And video viewers watching a specific program they've downloaded are likely to be more attentive.

The ultimate takeaway? There's nothing wrong with making branding ad buys, especially online where clutter is less prevalent. You can buy entire video series for sponsorship, and prices are still comparatively low. (Note: while this was a live presentation, much of the information is archived online at NielsenWire; you'll find a summary here: http://blog.nielsen.com/nielsenwire/online_mobile/looking-at-lift-inside-onl ine-video-advertising/.)

Incorporating ROI into the Marketing Plan

To develop ROI, you need to work in all those other operational factors and formulas. You need to integrate data from your marketing expenditures with sales data. Here's how to do it.

1. Gather all your factors for each profit center.
2. Set a target or goal for each profit center.
3. Set a benchmark and milestones (proxy measures) for each profit center.
4. Execute the plans.
5. Review the results.
6. Take action to improve your ROI.

(*Aside:* Most marketers will agree there's a mini-step we might call 3.5: testing the plan, the campaign, or the program before full execution. One of the areas that online marketing shines in is the capacity for multivariate testing that can provide oodles of data to optimize a campaign before full launch. For more on what's new in multivariate testing, see Chapter 6.)

Step 1: Gather the Factors

Pull together the numbers you'll need to determine both the *marketing investment* and *net revenues* figures to set up your ROI equations. The more accurate your numbers, the better you'll do (see the Special Section "ROI Basics" at the end of Chapter 7 if you need help on this).

Step 2: Set a Goal

Marketing ROI goals are typically set in percentages; we think it helps to also set more concrete goals. Units sold, hours billed, daily, monthly, quarterly, or annual revenue targets are all good. The ultimate goal is a ROI document that anyone in any department can understand. Hard unit numbers are understandable by all stakeholders in manufacturing, sales, marketing, public relations and finance, and even by your rank-and-file employees. If one of your goals is to establish a ROI-thinking culture throughout your organization, go this route.

Not good: goals such as "increase website traffic by X percent" or "improve click-through of banner ads by X percent." Those are not ROI goals, they're good intentions, possibly useful milestones. Good intentions—even milestones—don't pay for factory materials, floor space, or the salaries of the marketing staff.

As mentioned, this kind of data serves best when viewed only as proxy measures, indicators that help point direction. Online marketers sometimes refer to these as milestones. In this view, achieving 40,000 unique visitors to a website each month would be a milestone on the way to the goal. Tracking the click-through rate (CTR) of a banner ad, or how many visitors actually bought a product (say, 13,000 out of 40,000) are two more milestones that may be rendered in percentages, with a view to seeing, from a sales perspective, how things are moving along.

The goal, however, should be expressed in concrete terms: $300,000 in goods sold to the 13,000 visitors who actually purchased something.

In digital marketing lingo (or "webspeak," as some would say), the goal is sometimes referred to as a *conversion*, but "conversion" can mean many things on the web. But conversion must reflect the desired outcome of the entire campaign. Usually, conversions would be items sold. For a nonprofit website, however, the goal might be the number of visitors to a web page that describes the organization's work or philosophy, and 40,000 per month might indeed be the goal. But still, if the goal of the campaign were to get the visitors to purchase a T-shirt to help fund the nonprofit, then 13,000 (number of T-shirts sold) is the conversion, and the percentage (40,000 / 13,000 = 30.7 percent) is the conversion rate.

In the e-commerce arena, tracking the click-through rate on a banner ad is a fairly useless metric, merely a milestone on the way to conversions. But when the goal of the campaign is information— simply getting the word out online about your enterprise—then tracking the CTR becomes important if increasing the number of site visitors is actually the entire goal. The marketing manager can track and compare click-through rates through various campaign initiatives, and A/B test the effectiveness of banner placements on one set of URLs versus another, or compare CTR results from different treatments of text, images, and calls to action.

A good starting point is to set a goal for each profit center in terms of the expected revenue, and then create a set of milestones and a benchmark that can effectively measure effort and progress toward the goal. In most organizations, the marketing manager is given a specific goal from higher up. You should be free to create your own set of milestones and benchmarks, remembering always that these statistics will probably also be reviewed by C-suite suits.

Consider writing down a "snapshot" of your organization's current communications efforts at this moment in time. It can include an overview of your sector, any recent changes in government regulations that may affect your operations, such as shipping or mailing restrictions. Note your position in your marketplace and assess your main competitors for hearts, minds, and wallets. This will be useful later on if you need to create an executive summary, and can help keep you keyed into the bigger picture while you sharpen your marketing plan.

Step 3: Set Benchmarks and Milestones

This is where to put those soft metrics and your proxy measures. Visitors to a website, ad impressions, the number of new customers generated from flyer inserts placed in a convention goodie bag—it's all stuff you've sent out and can track a result for.

Some of these milestones will be data from your agency, if you use one: those fuzzy soft metrics of reach, frequency, or gross rating points if you use traditional media; if you're using online media these are the columns to place items such as page views, unique visitors, time spent on site, and conversion events such as click-throughs, downloads, registrations, and your expected conversion, which may be sales leads, actual sales, or other actions specified in your goals.

Rest assured that you don't need a ton of data to create benchmarks, even if yours is a new enterprise with no marketing history. Or if you haven't got all the data you think you need. As one of our favorite metrics gurus, Jim Sterne, often says, "even if your yardstick is two and a half feet long, you can still measure with it." If you sold 437 widgets or registered 437 e-mail addresses in the last quarter, that's a benchmark you can use.

At this point it can be useful to look at other organizations similar to yours, to determine what their success rates are. Don't be too discouraged if a larger entity has a success beyond your abilities. One of our friends in the digital book business was only slightly dismayed to find out that the newest title from Dan Brown (author of *The DaVinci Code*) sold 100,000 copies in digital form on its first on-sale day. Is that a goal? No. But it can be a benchmark, and there's nothing wrong with pursuing the best you can be.

One of the great things about using Google Analytics is that their website analysis tools are used by thousands of websites. In Figure 5-4 they show how our example website is fairing against websites of similar size. Obviously it's doing quite well. The closer you can get to statistics for websites for companies that are in your industry, however, the better your benchmark will stand up to scrutiny.

Figure 5-4. Benchmarks in Google Analytics.

Comparing: **All sites of similar size** (?) Open category list

For those who are familiar with Six Sigma financials, benchmarking by looking at websites of competitors is a common method. You select the best in class from your industry sector, and basically haunt the web to find their data. A source many overlook are foreign companies with similar products; again thanks to the web it's possible to find stellar companies not yet competing in your market area. The same holds true for organizations localized within the United States. If you own a steak restaurant in a small town, start looking at the web news for steak restaurants in major cities to find out not just what promotions they are doing, but how they are doing (chowhound.com is one national source of pithy reviews). Don't limit yourself to Google or Bing or Yahoo! when you search. Journalists routinely bypass these for the venerable search engine at www.lycos.com (first a project of Carnegie Mellon University, now owned by Korean communications firm Daum) and www.dogpile.com, which aggregates search from Google, Yahoo!, Bing, and others, and is often the most updated of the group.

On the web, benchmarking can focus on key indicators, the positive ones such as conversions, sign-ups, and percentage of repeat visits or time spent on site, and the negative ones, such as bounce rate (prospects leaving before converting) and shopping cart abandonment. Improving your negatives, whether online or at the checkout counter in a brick-and-mortar store, are an important, if secondary, goal of your marketing efforts. It will do you no good to have your marketing campaigns result in a flood of new prospects to your store or your website, if your customers are greeted by shoddy service. This is another area to monitor, because while you may not have control over these areas, it will certainly affect your ROI. Your best defense in the C-suite may be to have documentation of where, in the sales funnel, your efforts have gone to naught.

Step 4: Project, Then Execute

By all means pre-test key elements of your campaigns, even if your resources preclude anything but setting up panels of your friends and relatives (Step 3.5, remember?).

Remember that "intent to buy" isn't the same as "I bought." A handy rough estimate to gauge optimistic polling is to divide the response rates by five: if 100 people say they like the concept, don't assume more than twenty will act on that response.

A/B testing can go on forever, but the trend now is to test a few key elements at the start, and then continue to test as you go. Amazon.com watchers have noted the web giant frequently tests up to twenty elements on its home page in real time.

Bill Nussey, CEO of Silverpop, an Atlanta-based e-mail marketing firm, always has a few good points on how to test e-mails. His main advice is to split your list, and first test to a small subset of each of the two groups. The most common tests for e-mail are the following:

► Tests of landing pages linked to the e-mail.

► Tests of subject lines.

► Tests of personalization (works in some industries, not others).

► Long copy with images, versus short copy, no images.

None of this is new to direct-response marketers, but we've noticed you don't see A/B testing for Twitter campaigns or blog outreach. Too bad, as some interesting research is being done in this area. Blogger Dustin Curtis may not be a household name, but he was savvy enough to run a series of A/B tests of Twitter invite language on a group of 5,000 randomly selected visitors one single day. Here are the results by percentage of click-through rates, from some fairly common calls to action on the networking site:

"I'm on Twitter": 4.7 percent

"Follow me on Twitter": 7.3 percent

"You should follow me on Twitter": 10.9 percent

"You should follow me on Twitter here": 12.81 percent

Knowing that the more directive language resulted in higher click-through rates may be of use to any reader, and these results certainly bolster the notion that all elements of a campaign may be tested and made more efficient.

Step 5: Review the Results

Even the best analytics programs are faulty. While we don't see the point of believing all the results presented by an agency with a stake in perceived progress, we also don't believe you should take your successes, or your failures, at face value. Jim Sterne's strongest advice is always "look for the anomalies." Is that spike in sales a result of your genius ad copy or a factor beyond your control? Devote some time in the aftermath of every campaign to identifying areas that show some promise for future activity, and to quantify efforts that seemed to go nowhere. Reassessing results in a three- to six-month time frame can also be of use, as many campaigns take that long to reach customer consciousness, especially if your brand is not a familiar one.

Computerized campaigns that count click-throughs and other soft metrics should also be backed up with duplicate study, where applicable. A typical strategy for companies that use paid services to track online behaviors is to use free services as a backup. Google's free services for online marketers are described in Chapter 6, as are those of independent survey companies that can help you determine whether you are reaching your milestones, benchmarks, or goals.

Step 6: Take Action to Improve Your ROI

If you find some of your initiatives are not performing as well as you hoped, check under the hood and try to fix the problem before axing a program from your budget or summarily firing your agency. All too often the bottleneck or obstacle lurks at the bottom of the sales funnel. The obstacle may be financial (the customer balks at a high shipping cost) or material (the product is out of stock), or something you would never have imagined.

Or some part of the sales process is an information failure. Perhaps the sales team doesn't have access to revised product specs, or was not given sufficient notice of a special sale or promotion. Or it's financial there as well: the audience you've been wooing on Facebook or local radio doesn't really have the money to purchase your offering. There's nothing wrong with aspirational advertising—of the millions who see branding advertisements for DeBeers or Lexus, over the years some will eventually purchase a diamond or a sedan. Your ROI may be fine for a branding campaign, but you may find you need another set of initiatives you can track to see if you are on target for short-term goals.

The solutions are there. Offering a choice of shipping services may be a pain to your procurement department, but can help seal the deal, and be less expensive than offering "free shipping."

Another solution can be found in the Ace Hardware Case Study (end of Chapter 1), which shows the merits of in-store pickup as an alternative to delivery fees. Out-of-stock product is a common cause of lost sales. Take a look at LLBean.com's offerings of sport clothing;

their website (and their catalog call center) can alert customers that a particular shirt in size Medium is no longer available in light blue but still available in dark blue, a reasonable second choice that may save the sale. (Can your call center do that?)

Online, the biggest culprit is navigation issues. Is it easy to search for a product if you don't know the exact SKU, product number, or name? Is the registration process for new customers cumbersome or intrusive? One business services company saw its online conversions improve by 25 percent when it dropped the form field asking for a telephone number.

Routine diagnostics that cost little are online customer satisfaction surveys, and making Live Chat available. One financial services company we know saw its conversion shoot up when it added "live person" capability to its website. A small pharmaceutical supply house opted for 24-hour phone support, and plastered the number on its website, its catalog, order forms, and brochures. Four people were trained and took shifts in the early days; by the time the supply firm had graduated to hiring an external call center, it got itself sold (for a handsome sum) to a larger competitor.

Most of the fixes will boil down to customer care issues. Others will be strictly your fault. Did you blow a deadline for an insertion? Does the advertisement omit a call to action, or omit a number to call? Is the ad execution shoddy or unclear? Were copies of the new ad distributed to the sales team? Call your own team together, identify the problem, take responsibility, and move on.

A Look at Multi-Channel ROI in Practice

For our Hypothetical Company A, Jane, the marketing manager, has divided her profit centers by marketing channel. Thus, Jane's list of profit centers looks like this:

1. Direct sales through company website.
2. Direct sales by mail order catalog.
3. Direct sales by physical storefront A (Portland).
4. Direct sales by physical storefront B (San Diego).
5. Direct sales by third-party strategic partner (large national store chain).

Anita, Jane's assistant marketing manager, is specifically responsible for online sales promotions that relate to the company's website. Yet, at the same time, anything she does online is expected to enhance the sales through the other four channels, including the department store channel.

Every initiative Anita budgets has to generate revenue to meet goals that are set by Jane for each quarter of the business year. So, first, Anita will divide her yearly goal by the quarter, and further divide her planned web initiatives into separate profit centers. Her group, for each quarter, might look like this (see Figure 5–5):

1. Ongoing banner ad program.
2. Ongoing paid search program.
3. Special holiday banner promotion #1.
4. Special holiday banner promotion #2.
5. Facebook discount promotion #1.
6. Facebook discount promotion #2.
7. Twitter promotion for new product line.
8. YouTube promotion for new product line.
9. E-mail newsletter promotion month 1.
10. E-mail newsletter promotion month 2.
11. E-mail newsletter promotion month 3.
12. Special newsletter promotion for new product line.

Anita may view each of the twelve items above as an expense; if she is smart, like Jane, she will realize that each of the twelve is, in fact, a profit center. Each of the items is expected to generate a quantifiable increase in revenues through direct sales at the company's website. And, oh, yes, expected to enhance the revenues of Jane's four specified channels (catalog mail order, two retail outlets, and a department store chain) by brand building online.

To determine the ROI of her online campaigns, Anita will need a way to attribute revenue from each of her campaigns to the various channels beyond the website. Like Jane she may rely on coupon coding and tracking tags to automate the attributions, and in her own case, use web analytics to view activity on a day-to-day basis for each of her initiatives.

For budgeting and planning, both Jane and Anita can use the Dupont Formula (Chapter 2) as well as a classic predictive ROI projection (Chapter 2) to allocate assets to each of their profit centers, and come up with reasonable revenue targets and goals, based on logical benchmarks and industry intelligence.

Clearly, it's going to be easier for Jane to develop and determine ROI for each of these profit centers, provided she has access to at least monthly as well as quarterly and year-end sales data from each channel.

But the types of promotions Jane budgets for each profit center will differ, because the existing customer base and the prospective new customer base for each one is slightly different. For example, website and catalog customers tend to be self-sufficient buyers, requiring little more than a FAQ page for a twenty-four-hour customer service hotline to meet their expectations. Usually, these customers need only the prod or reminder of a special deal or new product, and this can be accomplished by e-mail or direct mail, or a promotional placement in

Figure 5-5. An online campaign budget with multi-channel components.

Web Sales Budget 2011

Web Sales Budget 2011	250,000					
Total Expenses	16,000	12,000	23,000	16,000	14,000	29,000
Projected End Balance	234,000	222,000	199,000	183,000	169,000	140,000

		Nov	Dec	Jan	Feb	Mar	Apr
	Media (Search + Display)						
PC1	Ongoing Banner Promotion (PPC)	0	0	5,000	5,000	2,000	2,000
PC2	Paid Search	0	0	5,000	0	0	0
PC3	Holiday Banner Special #1	10,000	10,000	0	0	0	0
PC4	HOLIDAY BANNER SPECIAL #2	0	1,000	1,000	0	0	1,000
	Social Media ads	0	0	0	2,000	0	1,000
	Total Media (Search + Display)	10,000	11,000	11,000	7,000	2,000	4,000
	Social Media Promotions						
PC5	FaceBook Discount Promotion #1	0	0	4,000	0	0	0
PC6	FaceBook Discount Promotion #2	0	0	0	0	4,000	0
PC7	Twitter Discount Promotion NPLaunch	0	0	0	0	0	5,000
PC8	YouTube Promotion NP Launch	0	0	0	0	0	2,000
	Total Social Media Promotions	0	0	4,000	0	4,000	7,000
	Marketing Communications						
PC 9	Email Coupon Promo Segment 1	0	0	3,000	3,000	3,000	3,000
PC 10	Email Coupon Promo Segment 2	0	0	2,000	1,000	2,000	2,000
PC 11	Special Email Coupon NP Launch	0	0	0	0	0	10,000
PC 12	Email Coupon Promo Segment 3	1,000	1,000	1,000	1,000	1,000	1,000
	Other	0	0	0	0	0	0
	Total Marketing Communications	1,000	1,000	6,000	5,000	6,000	16,000
	MultiChannel Support Promo						
	Catalog Support Promotions (partial)	5,000	0	0	0	0	0
	Portland Store Special Promo	0	0	0	0	0	0
	San Diego Store Promo	0	0	1,000	1,000	0	0
	Store Chain Promo (partial)	0	0	1,000	2,000	1,000	1,000
	Store Chain Promo (partial)	0	0	0	1,000	1,000	1,000
	Other	0	0	0	0	0	0
	Total MultiChannel Support Promo	5,000	0	2,000	4,000	2,000	2,000

a publication or website known to attract these buyers. Outreach to new customers may be a mix of digital and print promotions as well, with a typical offer of a free sample or new-customer discount coupon to generate the leads.

In-store customers may expect more support during the purchase, and buying patterns may be influenced by the skill of sales staff at these locations. To attract new customers at ground level, Jane has many options: local media would now include local mobile device promotions that involve texting or geocentric advertising, as well as local spots on national TV or radio programs, along with local print, local mailers, and promotions that attract community and local press, such as charity events.

Jane also has the option to promote more than one profit center in a single promotional campaign. A print ad can feature the local store as well as the website; a web banner campaign that directs a browser to the company website will also display the locations of the two stores (more finely if the web ads are also geo-targeted). Or the web ads may be co-op and the cost split with the national chain. If this is the case, Jane can still pin down which revenue came from which part of a campaign, if codes are used on coupons and tags used to track online clicks to an attributable conversion point.

So both Jane and Anita will use traditional finance methods and the latest in customer-tracking metrics to pursue their goals.

A few floors above Jane and Anita's office suite, the company CFO just finished a lovely lunch with the CEO, and she has determined new revenue goals for the coming year: 20 percent growth, or perhaps 5 percent growth every quarter. The CFO may be dimly aware, as Jane is fully aware, that the San Diego retail store has been lagging in revenue for months. The CFO isn't going to care if Anita can score a record-breaking 23 percent open rate on her new-product e-mail, although she may hear it through the grapevine if the celebrity You-Tube video tanks.

Yet Anita, Jane, and the CFO can embark on their new mission, calmly and well fitted with information tools and reporting techniques that will make both their failures and their successes strategic learning experiences. Everyone, this time, is going to confidently manage their marketing by their numbers.

Tools for Measuring Online Performance to Maximize ROI

IN THIS CHAPTER, we'll look specifically at online tools and how they can be integrated with sales and CRM databases, to extract the numbers you need for calculating the ROI of your marketing expenses. We find many marketers are not as familiar as they'd like to be with these tools. Rather than hand the whole responsibility to your IT department or your ad agency, you should understand the limits and capabilities available to you today.

There are many free tools and programs online to measure your *marketing investment* and assist in determining some of your *net revenue* numbers. We'll go over the main products available in North America, tell you what you'll be getting for your money, and then discuss how to align the resulting outpouring of statistics with your marketing goals.

There are myriad online software tools for measuring web activity available from a variety of competing vendors. And unfortunately, like most competitive software products, they are largely incompatible with each other. While prices range from free to expensive, some of these don't always provide meaningful data, and most are useless unless you've got a human being somewhere in your company who can make sense out of the stats. Consistently we are told that money is spent disproportionately on technology at the expense of human analysis, and in fact many enterprise consultants heartily recommend that, when you make an investment in analytics tools, you match those dollars with salary dollars for staff.

Metrics tools fall into several categories, principally site side or ad server side. Site side metrics are those measured by the servers of the website or content company on whose pages ads appear.

Ad server side metrics are measured at the servers of the third-party ad serving company. These are companies like DoubleClick and Atlas, which actually serve the ad that you see. You might not think there would be a disparity between the metrics from these two sources, website and ad server, but you would be wrong. The metrics rarely agree.

For specific campaigns, there are measurement tools for social media, online videos, and other marketing niches. These include software programs that attempt to measure soft data such as "engagement" or "sentiment." If you're interested in seeing how your efforts compare against competitors, there are independent agencies—Neilsen being the newest—that rank your traffic and status within your market sector.

In the main, these tools do not easily integrate with one another, and none offers a complete cross-media solution. There are many dashboards out there that you can use, and more that you can build, but the first step to getting a comprehensive data is knowing what you can wring out of the tools you choose.

Site Side Analytics

There are a number of players in this field, but the two major ones are Omniture, the big dog in expensive site side analytics, and Google, which offers a robust free product. We discuss these first:

▶ **Omniture** (www.omniture.com). *The pedigree:* Omniture is based in Utah with offices worldwide and was purchased in 2009 by Adobe. Previously, it had bought behavioral targeting company Touch Clarity, web analytics company Visual Sciences, Inc. (formerly Web-SideStory), and Israeli e-commerce search solution provider Mercado.

The product: SiteCatalyst is Omniture's flagship web analytics application, with entry-level pricing for the small to mid-size enterprise. For just 1M page views, you are not likely to get much of a price break. Expect to pay a CPM of around $0.625. Average price to get started is about $5K per month.

The company has other offerings in search, data warehousing, enterprise search, and social media tracking, among other areas. Integrations with other systems are offered under the title "Genesis."

Once your site is wired to SiteCatalyst, you can easily analyze site traffic and e-commerce activity. A trending feature allows stats to be plotted over time. As the product is primarily aimed at e-commerce users, a separate section focuses on commerce reporting, with report categories showing conversions, shopping cart activity, and individual product performances (see Figure 6-1).

Even with the most basic edition of SiteCatalyst, there is a wide variety of trackable elements, under these broad categories:

► Conversion analysis.

► Path analysis.

► Visitor segmentation.

As with all site side tools, there are many ways to report user click patterns as they navigate your site. Increasingly it is possible to see the data (visitors, conversions, etc.) graphically via such powerful visioning tools such as Tableau (www.tableau.com). See Figure 6-1.

Figure 6-1. Detail of a SiteCatalyst report.

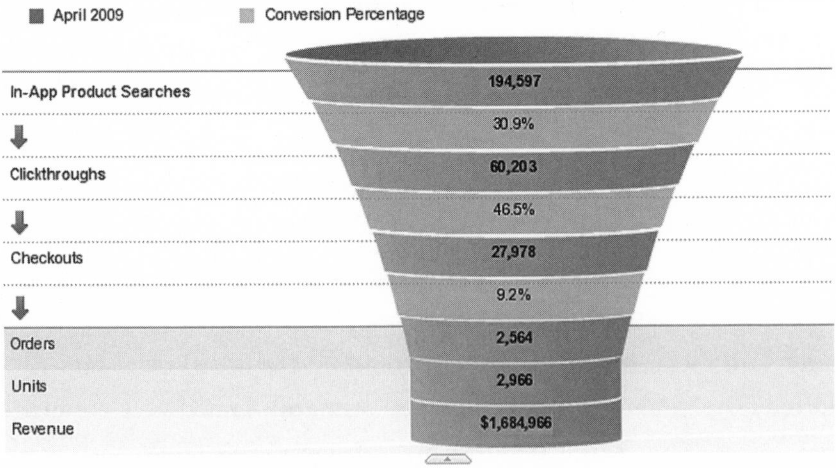

And all this can be reported in multiple ways and by easily variable criteria: dates, day parts, seasonality, and the like.

We expect to see Adobe exploit synergies with Omniture, probably integrating analytics into their web creation tools in the not-so-distant future.

A side note: Trip Chowdhry, analyst with Global Equities Research, has pointed out that the Omniture deal would provide Adobe with new ways to create revenue. It was a good deal for Omniture, too. Chowdhry said that Adobe paid almost twice what Omniture was worth because the company had been losing market share to Google Analytics. The analyst noted that Google Analytics offers a free web analytics service that isn't nearly as comprehensive as that of Omniture, but it's hard for companies to justify the expense of Omniture when Google offers something serviceable for free.

Which brings us to the freebie itself.

▶ **Google Analytics** (http://www.google.com/analytics/). *The pedigree:* Google Analytics is a free product from Google that provides an exceptional amount of visitor data. It results from Google's acquisition of Urchin Software. Google rolled out its branded analytics service in 2005 and has provided several subsequent updates. It differs from some of its competitors in that it's aimed at marketers rather than webmasters and of course excels at manipulating data from Google's own AdWords and AdSense programs.

In its ongoing quest for world domination, the Google gang gives analytics away free just as it loses money on bandwidth serving You-Tube (to the tune of half a billion dollars a year according to some sources). Google wants to be your default provider of anything ad related (and many initiatives far beyond). So long as its core search business continues to gush money to its bottom line, Google can be expected to continue to support such ventures. Accordingly, one should feel emboldened to use Google Analytics without fear that Google will suddenly jack up the price, to an actual price.

The product: Google Analytics can track visitors from all sources, including display advertising, search engines, e-mail marketing campaigns, PPC networks, and links within PDF documents that are being read on a web-enabled computer screen. Google Analytics offers a high-level dashboard view as well as comprehensive data in reports (Figure 6-2). Users can track such goals as sales, leads, page views, and downloads, and can use the information to optimize campaigns.

Advanced features include:

▶ Tracking sales, conversions, and soft metrics against threshold or benchmark levels that you define.

▶ Integration with AdWords and AdSense programs, with post-click data on your keywords, search queries, match type, and more. The AdSense reports show publishers which site content generates the most revenue.

Figure 6-2. Detail of a Google Analytics report.

Advertising ROI

AdWords sent 6,470 visits via 4 campaigns

Visits	Impressions	Clicks	Cost	CTR	CPC	RPC	ROI	Margin
6,470	1,305,625	25,016	$10,011.48	1.92%	$0.40	$0.16	-61.09%	-157.02%
% of Site Total 3.33%	% of Site Total 100.00%	% of Site Total 100.00%	% of Site Total 100.00%	Site Avg. 1.92% (0.00%)	Site Avg. $0.40 (0.00%)	Site Avg. $0.51 (-69.53%)	Site Avg. $27.68% (-320.70%)	Site Avg. 21.68% (-824.25%)

Campaign	Visits	Impressions	Clicks	Cost	CTR	CPC	RPC	ROI	Margin
1. Google Store: English-Americas	6,384	102,147	8,902	$3,106.73	8.71%	$0.36	$0.44	25.38%	20.24%
2. (not set)	75	0	0	$0.00	0.00%	$0.00	$0.00	0.00%	0.00%
3. Newbie Campaign	11	19,041	200	$187.72	1.05%	$0.94	$0.00	100.00%	0.00%
4. Google Store: English-EU, APAC & ROW	0	1,184,437	15,914	$8,717.03	1.34%	$0.42	$0.00	100.00%	0.00%

► Campaign tracking for branding measures (reach, impressions) that can track e-mail campaigns with banner ads, offline ads, and more.

► E-commerce reporting functions that allow you to trace transactions to campaigns and keywords.

► Cross-channel and multimedia tracking allows you to track mobile websites, mobile apps, and web-enabled mobile devices, including both high-end and non-JavaScript–enabled phones. You can also track usage of your Ajax, Flash, social networking, and Web 2.0 applications.

► Benchmarking data allows you to find out whether your site usage metrics underperform or outperform those of your industry. Opt-in benchmarking compares your key metrics against aggregate performance metrics while preserving the confidentiality of your data.

► A variety of options of in-site analysis allow you to isolate and compare subsets of your traffic, with rubrics such as "Paid Traffic" and "Visits with Conversions" or customized views that apply to your industry or campaign.

► Customized reports (for the C-suite) and customized dashboards (for you) are also available, with pivot tables, multiple dimensions, and filtering features. Funnel-shaped conversion funnels and on-the-fly tools let you manipulate data right in the report tables. The reports can be exported into a variety of spreadsheets, and even e-mailed on an automated basis to your personalized list.

Google Analytics also monitors your reports and automatically alerts you of anomalies in data patterns. You can also set up custom alerts to notify you when specific thresholds are reached. Some recent innovations are 3-D report renderings, and geo-targeting that is useful for brick-and-mortar analysis. We also like the ability to see where customers go after they leave your site, which can highlight weaknesses in marketing or fulfillment.

Google has taken the lead in offering not just page activity metrics and tagging but also event tagging. As new programming languages like Ajax allow user engagement to take place without pages being refreshed, such tagging schemes would seem to be the way of the future.

TAGS AND COOKIES

An issue that often comes up with Google is privacy. The company uses its own first-party cookies. While Google itself tracks your visitors at every step, data collection from your customers is not shared with other organizations at this time. Most metrics tools are implemented by including a "page tag." In Google, for example, this is referred to as the Google Analytics Tracking Code (GATC). Once a site adds this hidden snippet of JavaScript code to every page, this code collects visitor data and sends it to Google (or another analytics system) as well as setting a first-party cookie on each visitor's computer. The cookie allows the site to know whether the visitor has been there before and where he or she came from.

That is how the system divides your website visitors into categories, typically:

► *Total visits.*
► *Unique visitors.*
► *Returned or Registered Returning visitors.*

Cookie tracking is hardly foolproof. There is evidence that a small but important audience segment will delete these cookies, thereby skewing visitor data. This problem is common to most analytics software and is getting worse as privacy issues become more important to computer users, and users in general become more savvy in removing their cookie crumb trails. Datran Media, which monitors behavioral targeting on the web, has estimated that between 30 percent and 50 percent of all Internet users regularly delete their cookies.

So when does Google suffice? And when is it necessary or advisable to buy into a premium tool like Omniture and forego the free product?

Clearly Omniture is aimed at the larger e-commerce website. It offers a high degree of customization and support and many experts who are adept at complicated implementations. Google is aimed at the marketer who does not need a high degree of customization; the downside is that Google's rather robust software takes too much of a "one size fits all" approach.

This is not to say that Google Analytics lacks support: Google provides direct e-mail support in many languages and a user can contact the Google Analytics Support team, the Google Analytics Help website, or can visit the Analytics Help Forum. Google has created a network of Google Analytics Authorized Consultants (GAACs) for more advanced consultations and implementations. However, the infrastructure of support for customizing Omniture remains more robust than that for Google Analytics.

And, there are other choices also worth looking into.

▶ **Web Trends Enterprise Suite** (www.webtrends.com). *The pedigree:* Webtrends, Inc., provides web analytics and other software solutions related to marketing intelligence. The company was founded in 1993 and now serves more than 10,000 large and small firms.

In 2009, Webtrends launched a transit ad campaign revolving around the question of whether or not cyclists should pay a road tax.

The ad asked, "Should cyclists pay a road tax?" The campaign ignited a furor and a controversy. Both drivers and cyclists reacted hotly to the question. The community reacted strongly to the ad, with strident opinion on both sides. What was the goal? The campaign aim was solely to demonstrate the ability of the company's web analytics to track the resulting online commentary around the issue.

The product: Along with its core Analytics software, Webtrends offers related products including Analytics for Facebook, Social Measurement, Marketing Warehouse, and Visitor Intelligence. The analytics tool (Analytics 9) collects data from your web server log files augmented with information from client-side scripts.

The Webtrends Open Exchange is a network of related marketing technologies—ad serving, content management, customer relationship management, e-mail marketing, enterprise campaign management, site search, targeting and optimization, user experience, and website monitoring.

▶ **Coremetrics** (www.coremetrics.com). *The pedigree*: founded in 1999, Coremetrics received the highest score for customer satisfaction in Forrester Research's Wave Report in 2009.

The product: Coremetrics helps companies measure and improve the effectiveness of online marketing programs with tools that include search engine bid management, e-mail targeting, ad impression attribution, and cross-sell recommendations. Coremetrics touts its Continuous Optimization Platform as a unique system that addresses the need to more successfully convert and retain customers online. At the heart of the platform is Coremetrics' Lifetime Individual Visitor Experience (LIVE) Profile, which tracks a customer's browsing behavior over the long term, including offline information, not just the first or last click.

The amount of customization is considerable, and extends across e-mail, website, and ad network data.

▶ **Unica** (www.unica.com). This global marketing solutions company purchased several smaller firms to create a broad array of turnkey technical services available for CRM-based web analytics. Unica Net-Insight is the primary product, which may be customized for very large organizations from a vast menu of options.

▶ **Clicky** (www.getclicky.com). Clicky Web Analytics is a product of Roxr Software, founded in Portland in 2006. This newcomer provides a free web analytics service to monitor basic data, and the main product is well suited to the individual or small enterprise. A few tricks from this pony are site monitoring via your iPhone and good reporting of Flash.

Dashboards for Net Revenue Data

Many vendors of custom dashboards supply real-time statistics for the key users of analytics data, whether they be CEO, CFO, VP, or sales manager. You can easily set up key performance indicators, also known as KPI, as needed. Let's take another look at the dashboard from Unica's Netsight, which we first saw in Chapter 4 (see Figure 6-3).

Good dashboards allow users to look backwards in time at data. Why would you want to do that? There are many reasons; you might, for example, want to determine seasonal trends. Or you might want to examine the performance of a long-term branding campaign to determine if it's time to refresh the message to attract a new customer group. Figure 6-4 on page 161 contains a snapshot showing when most high-value customers came to a site.

Figure 6-3. Unica's dashboard.

Many use web analytics do "multivariate" testing, as well as A/B testing. This can be one of the most important uses of web analytics. Unica NetInsight makes A/B testing easy. A screen shot appears in Figure 6-5 on page 162. In this example, two different landing pages, with different messages, are being compared.

Offline Marketing Insights

The power of dashboarding is a big assist if your organization has multiple sales channels all benefiting from cross-channel campaigns. Here's another example from NetInsight that illustrates how you can

Figure 6-4. Filtered analytics chart.

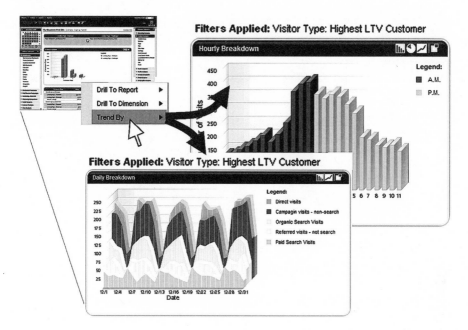

segment your online reports using offline data. The screen shot in Figure 6-6 on page 163 shows customers based on their lifetime value range, including both online and offline purchases.

Third-Party Ad Server Analytics

Ad reporting systems are vital to websites that sell advertising, as well as necessary to marketing departments that are purchasing online advertising space to drive traffic, leads, or direct sales. Not surprisingly, this is the most mature area of web statistics software, even though its yield—impressions and click-through rates and the like—may repre-

Figure 6-5. Multivariate testing.

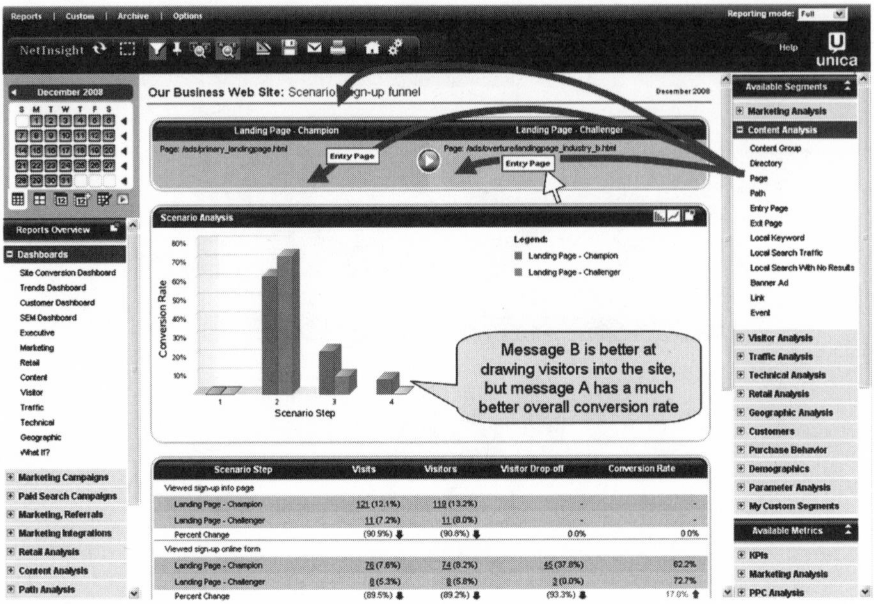

sent only proxy measures, or at best, provide the background for marketing investment cost accounting.

Many professionals, including Mediasmith's director of analytics Michael Andrew, counsel that there is always the need to reconcile site side data provided by systems like Omniture with ad server side data like that provided by DoubleClick.

Here's a short roster of major third-party suppliers:

▶ **DoubleClick DART** (www.doubleclick.com). *The pedigree:* DoubleClick, one of the early forces in web advertising, focuses on

Figure 6-6. Segmenting customers by lifetime value (LTV).

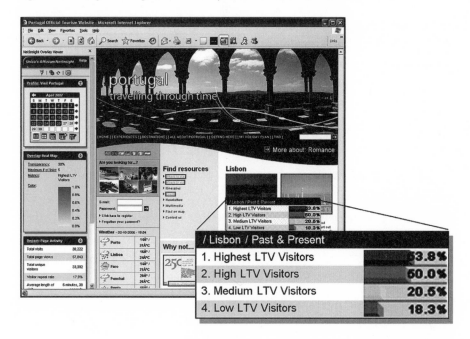

uploading and serving ads on behalf of web publisher clients, and measuring performance. Google acquired DoubleClick in 2008, for $3.1 billion in cash. Clients are primarily ad agencies and media companies who use the technology to target ads to users and to deliver and report on those campaigns. The principal product, known as DART, is used by advertisers and publishers. DART for Advertisers (DFA) automates the ad buying process for advertisers and agencies. DART for Publishers (DFP) automates the management of ad inventory.

The product: The company offers a search management product that includes a bid management system as well as campaign administration tools. Like other vendors, DoubleClick depends on cookie data to accomplish its user targeting goals.

► **Atlas Solutions** (www.atlassolutions.com). *The pedigree*: The Atlas platform has been around since 1997, and was acquired by Microsoft ten years later as part of its $6 billion purchase of Aquantive. Like DoubleClick, Atlas offers third-party ad serving and analytics. It provides digital media technologies for agencies, advertisers, and publishers. The solutions for agencies and advertisers attempt unified management of digital marketing campaigns across display banners, rich media, search, video, and websites.

The product: Atlas competes head to head with DoubleClick and offers a similar range of products including search management and bid management systems, a media console for planning and reporting, and ad services for rich media, video, and custom research. Atlas Advanced Analytics features whatever's current, and this company is a leader in what it calls "engagement mapping"—tracking customers backwards through the sales funnel, to view banners and sites visited before purchase. The Atlas Institute, well funded by Microsoft, provides frequent reports and studies on issues such as click attribution.

► **Eye Blaster** (www.eyeblaster.com). *The pedigree*: Eyeblaster began as a rich media technology and has evolved into a full-fledged competitor for Atlas and DoubleClick. Its solution suites manage campaigns across digital media channels, including online, mobile, and in-game, and across a variety of formats, including rich media, in-stream video, display, and search.

The product: MediaMind is a cross-channel ad serving system with the smaller enterprise in mind: reports can be displayed as dashboards, summarized in PowerPoint or Excel with plug-ins, and customized depending on your media.

Search Tools

Kenshoo, Clickable, and Marin Software offer search marketing tools and analytics. They incorporate bid management and campaign administration for clients running substantial paid search campaigns. Bob's Toolbox, on the book's website (http://www.marketingbythe numbers.com), lists many more.

The variety of companies offering search tools reflects a decade of mature search theory. Back when Yahoo was a major search player, bid management software evolved that was able to "game the system." This was because Yahoo displayed the bidding landscape and enabled tactics to "jam" other bidders. The dominance of Google ended the game playing, as Google was opaque as to the bidding landscape. The current bidding technologies therefore now offer robust "housekeeping" and administrative capacity, but lack the capacity to manipulate the competitive bidding process. Consequently, your selection of a vendor is more likely to be concerned with price and a good mesh with your organization's online operations.

Video Distribution and Measurement

As web video occupies a larger share of the digital experience, tools have evolved to upload and track the play of these videos.

▶ **Tube Mogul** (www.tubemogul.com). *The pedigree:* Tube Mogul is a free service (with a fee-based upgrade that includes hosting services) through which you can upload your video into multiple websites and which helps you to track your video views. In December 2009 the company announced a partnership with video distribution platform Brightcove, and this year introduced Destinations, an improved version of its load-once-distribute-anywhere video platform. And it's still free. A popular destination among marketers is its daily "TubeMogul Top 40," which tracks the most viewed videos surveyed for the day. This is also available with free registration on the site.

The product: TubeMogul's InPlay (Figure 6-7) is a Flash-based analytics service that tracks audience statistics and user interaction in real time. Among the measurable parameters in the free service are viewed minutes, viewer attention, per-stream quality, syndication tracking, region tracking, player tracking, audience, and advertising.

► **Visible Measures** (www.visiblemeasures.com). *The pedigree*: Visible Measures specializes in measuring the consumption and distribution of Internet video. From a start in 2005, the Boston-based company's Hollywood connections are legend—for example, they cut a deal with the People's Choice Awards, becoming the "official Internet measurement partner" for the 2010 telecast. Almost as popular among viewers is its "Million Views Club" featuring top-rated and most watched videos online. Other useful charts are *Advertising Age*'s Top Ten Ad Campaigns, and *Variety*'s Top Ten Film Trailers.

The product: The company's video measurement solutions are powered by three core technologies, the Video Placement Multiplier, Viral Reach Database, and Video Metrics Engine. The Video Placement Multiplier uploads your videos to more than forty video-sharing sites in a single step while providing some control over brand placement. The Viral Reach Database gives visibility into viral video placements and audience growth by tracking what's currently online—more than 100 million videos across 150 + video-sharing destinations. The Video Metrics Engine processes its version of "viewer engagement"— with millions of video streams every day in real time, recording every interaction by every viewer from every video on the user's network.

Web Ratings and Market Comparison Stats

Marketing is a competitive game and it never hurts (though sometimes it is imperative) to know how your web enterprise stacks up against

Figure 6-7. Data samples from InPlay.

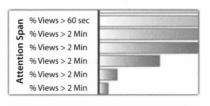

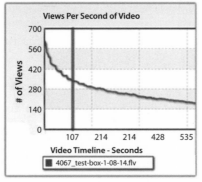

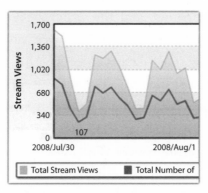

your direct competitors. Most independent web ratings firms issue periodic public reports you will find generally useful; if you want time-sensitive data, it may cost you.

▶ **Quantcast** (www.quantcast.com). *The pedigree:* This newcomer among rating services was launched three years ago by a team of Silicon Valley veterans.

The product: Quantcast is a website that is based on viewing the statistics of other web sites. Its prime focus is to analyze the sites in order to obtain accurate usage statistics by surfers from the United States. Participating websites insert Quantcast code inside web pages they wish to have included in statistics. This code allows Quantcast to keep track of the traffic directed toward those websites, providing some pretty thorough details about web pages created by competitors who are also participating, and the web pages of publisher sites or affiliate sites you might be interested in advertising on. This information includes demographic data such as whether the web visitor is a male or female, average income, the age group of the viewer, and the number of U.S. homes the website reaches. Quantcast compares and correlates information received from one participating publisher with another and generates inferences. The inferences are possible because the Quantcast code causes the user's browser to access Quantcast's servers. This allows capture of the user's IP address and information, and it returns cookies that are stored in the user's browser. Quantcast also reveals other popular sites that the average viewer browses, allowing you to discover your direct competitors online.

Any company can sign up for free to be "quantified." Over 20,000 publishers have agreed to place Quantcast's code on their sites, which allows them to get more accurate information about the types of people who use their site. Many also use the company's panel data service to build audience profiles—useful to any advertiser interested in seeing whether a magazine's website visitors differ from its print audience.

▶ **Nielsen** (www.nielsen.com). *The pedigree:* Nielsen Online provides measurement and analysis of online audiences, advertising, video, consumer-generated media, word of mouth, commerce, and consumer behavior. Previously a majority investor in both companies, Nielsen Inc. purchased NetRatings and BuzzMetrics, combining them to form Nielsen Online.

The products: As might be surmised, Nielsen (of TV and radio fame) provides a heady mix of audience measurement that's pricey to boot. Homescan Online, in partnership with Nielsen, measures both consumers' offline purchasing behavior and online surfing activity. Over the past year, this has been expanded to match purchasing behavior with ad exposure through various forms of television, including time-shifted DVR viewing and web video.

According to Randall Beard, executive vice president and general manager for CPG Advertising Solutions, another part of the Nielsen measurement empire, Nielson has launched four specific initiatives around cross-channel ROI.

The first initiative was the joint venture Nielsen has with Catalina that marries Catalina's loyalty card household data with Nielsen's viewing data. Hypothetically, says Beard, one could identify occasional Tide detergent users from the loyalty data and build media plans across multiple media that specifically targets them.

Second, the Nielsen IAG syndicated panel of 3 million consumers has response data for every TV ad and show for the last five years. The panel measures digital ad effectiveness and shows correlations with TV and radio consumption. Variables measured include website visitation via cookie data, along with soft metrics for ad recall and brand sentiment via survey. As Randall said, "Cross-media synergy is real. One and one does equal two and a half." TV and web combined was 35 percent more effective than either alone.

The third initiative, Nielsen's Home Scan panel, lets panel members use a wand to scan in CPG purchase info on the goods they buy. This panel tracks actual consumption. Plus, Nielsen knows what ads these people were exposed to, both on TV and digitally. This panel data has revealed that brands see measurable lift in consumption from their online branding activities. This is despite the fact that there is relatively low connection between click-through rates and consumption.

The fourth initiative involves Nielsen looking at the relative effectiveness of paid media (paid advertising) versus earned media (unpaid media mentions such as news items, blog postings, or social media buzz). "Earned" is being used here the way the PR industry has begun to use the term, as the "earned but not bought" result of search and social media marketing (as well as PR). Among the earned media channels measured are Twitter, Facebook, organic search, and website visitation.

Keep an eye on Nielsen, they may yet find a way to quantify buzz!

▶ **TRA** (www.traglobal.com). *The pedigree:* Launched in 2007, TRA is a ratings service that is challenging Nielsen's dominance in cross-channel ratings, linking TV ratings to product purchase behavior. MTV Networks has signed with TRA, which covers TRA data for all MTVN channels such as MTV, Comedy Central, VH1, TV Land, Spike, and Nickelodeon.

The product: Its second-by-second estimates are based on data from 1.5 million set-top-box households and product purchase data from 54 million households participating in shopper loyalty programs to create a single source panel of 370,000 households.

TRA has signed about a dozen clients in addition to MTV, including CBS, Group M, and MediaVest. MTV's Colleen Fahey Rush, EVP for strategic insights and research, notes that TRA provides a way for MTV's networks to avoid being pigeonholed by demographic, saying "Adding the layer of the purchase data is really going to differentiate the kinds of audiences and consumers we have across each of our brands compared to other channels. Our viewers are purchasing across a whole spectrum of categories. We want to show advertisers and agencies that our viewers put their money on the counter."

► **comScore** (www.comscore.com). *The pedigree:* comScore is an Internet marketing research company that offers large panels of Internet users to survey web behavior. Publicly held, it is an amalgam of acquired related technologies and companies and has lately been moving into Latin American markets with its 2009 acquisition of Certifica, which provides web measurement services in Chile, Argentina, Mexico, Brazil, Columbia, and Peru.

The products: As with the current Nielsen products, the surveys are automated: comScore maintains a group of users, estimated at 2 million, who have allowed monitoring software to be installed on their computers. comScore adjusts the statistics using weights to make sure that each population segment is adequately represented and is considered a reliable source of ratings data for comparative websites.

The company will sell you customized reports (pricey) but regularly publicizes data of interest to all sectors, such as the Media Metrix reports of top sites in a given month. A look at November 2009's highest traffic sites (see Figure 6–8) yielded an abundance of consumer data.

We show this chart because this is where advertisers could first

Figure 6-8. comScore Media Metrix, November 2009.

comScore Core Search Report*
November 2009 vs. October 2009
Total U.S.-Home, Work, and University Locations
Source: comScore qSearch

| | Share of Searches (%) | | |
| | | | Point Change |
Core Search Entity	Oct-09	Nov-09	Nov-09 vs. Oct-09
Total Core Search	*100.0%*	*100.0%*	*N/A*
Google Sites	65.4%	65.6%	0.2
Yahoo! Sites	18.0%	17.5%	− 0.5
Microsoft Sites	9.9%	10.3%	0.4
Ask Network	3.9%	3.8%	− 0.1
AOL LLOC Network	2.9%	2.8%	− 0.1

Based on the five major search engines including partner searches and cross-channel searches.

see the gain in Microsoft's search rankings—10 percent of all search requests (compared to Google's 65 percent) and a 0.04 percent increase over the previous month, as Bing replaced both Yahoo and Google as the default search engine on the newest PCs (Yahoo's share of search dropped 0.05 percent).

The ratings for the most active sites in November 2009 also revealed a rather fine snapshot of the U.S online consumer in the fourth quarter, and confirmed that the American buying public remained aspirational and hopeful as it entered the second holiday season of the brief recession (see Figure 6-9). The most trafficked site, with a gain of more than 3,000 percent from the previous month, was for Visa's Black Card, a credit card with a $495 annual fee. Shoppers also flocked to discounted sites for toys and games (Ubisoft, Game-Stop, and Toys 'R Us sites, and shopped for value online at Sears, Wal-Mart, and Best Buy. A surprising addition for the holiday was a

77 percent increase in visitors to Shoplocal.com, a shopping aggregator many used to track down competitive prices (on their web-enabled phones) while shopping in stores.

Some lesser-known players to assist with ad placement are worth knowing. They include:

NetView: An Internet audience measurement service that provides measurement and demographic data on Internet audiences.

AdRelevance: A service that captures advertising activity across all major industries, channels, and ad formats and across most ad types, including all major forms of rich media, on the Web.

Figure 6-9. Top gains for retail site use, November 2009.

comScore Top 10 Gaining Properties by Percentage Change in Unique Visitors* (U.S.)
November 2009 vs. October 2009
Total U.S.-Home, Work, and University Locations
Source: comScore Media Metrix

	Total Unique Visitors (000)		
	Oct-09	**Nov-09**	**% Change**
Total Internet: Total Audience	198,218	201,139	1
BlackCard.com	168	5,459	3,148
Ubisoft Entertainment	1,925	6,916	259
GameStop	5,871	11,349	93
Toys 'R Us Sites	8,111	14,794	82
ShopLocal.com	5,151	9,132	77
Best Buy Sites	16,141	26,943	67
Kohls Corporation	7,651	12,173	59
Grisoft	3,922	6,178	58
Wal-Mart	31,808	49,341	55
Sears Sites	17,143	26,299	53

Ranking based on the top 250 properties in November 2009. Excludes entities whose growth was primarily due to implementation of Media Metrix 360hybrid audience measurement.

The service also contains specific ad buyer contacts and rate card information.

@Plan: A target-marketing platform for Internet media planning, buying, and selling. It reports demographics, in-depth lifestyle, and brand preference data.

VideoCensus: Audience measurement and analysis of online video usage.

SiteCensus: A site-centric reporting system uses server-side-visit reports. It provides media companies and publishers with third-party measurement for web site analysis; newsletter and e-mail conversion tracking; ad and keyword measurement; and audience assessment.

Social Media and Soft Metrics

For those with an interest in proxy measures, innumerable service companies will be happy to let you pay them to track your buzz and analyze a universe of tweets. The following companies are making an effort to quantify soft metrics for addition into the sales funnel to help you track ROI. Whether you use their services or not, their activities are worth keeping track of, as they represent the cutting edge of social metrics at this time.

▶ **Radian6** (www.Radian6.com). Radian6 provides tools for real-time social media monitoring and analysis. The service is affordable, with a minimum of $500/month, that has made it a popular entry level for marketers of all stripes, though its usefulness may be less for marketers than for PR and ad agencies. Its social media monitoring platform tracks what is being said online about brands, organizations, and issues. The solution monitors all forms of social media, including blog sites, video-sharing sites, opinion review forums, photo-sharing sites, and new and emerging channels such as micro-blogging (Twitter). Multiple languages are supported including English, French, Italian, German, Simplified Chinese, Korean, and Japanese.

▶ **Sysomos** (www.sysomos.com). The main product is called MAP (Media Analysis Platform) and offerings include automated sentiment analysis, influencer tracking on social media, and geo-tracking.

▶ **Alterian** (www.alterian.com). Alterian SM2 is a social media monitoring product designed for public relations use, tracking brand conversation and measuring sentiment across social channels and providing comparative reviews with competitors. It is part of a larger suite of services that can be purchased individually or together as an integrated marketing platform.

Some Tips to Optimize Your Tools

Earlier this year, Bob had the chance talk with Gary Angel, the CEO of Semphonic, about metrics and ROI. Semphonic is one of the leading web analytics consultancies in the United States and their clients include companies like American Express, Genentech, Intuit, Kohler, Microsoft, Nokia, Sears, and *The Washington Post*.

Two of the big takeaways:

1. Test your tools.
2. Make sure you have the capability to fully segment not only your audience but your various touch points.

Take traffic, for example—it's one of the main soft metrics found at the top of many online sales funnels.

Gary points out that only a tiny fraction of web traffic comes direct. Direct traffic is now easily trackable, but what about the rest? For a major hard goods manufacturer, Semphonic set about to track brand awareness across many different media and to correlate that with econometric data, seasonality, and other factors. The media tracked included TV and radio buys by market, search, display, and print. Semphonic looked at what had an impact on site visitation and engagement and made an interesting discovery: TV had by far the biggest influence on site visitation. In fact, it was the only offline media that produced a statistically significant impact on traffic. As Gary said, "TV blew away radio and print." One other interesting fact—the correlations were strongest when time-lagged slightly—meaning that the full impact of media wasn't felt immediately.

They also noticed that search was very responsive to both earned and paid media. As search practitioners know, much search traffic is "branded search"—queries for specific brands. Gary suggests that this means that search may not be the customer acquisition tool that it is often thought of as, but instead is a response (and retention) mechanism for brand marketing in all its forms.

Gary notes that while the tools exist to measure ROI across media, to do so you need to "baseline" your site and your media efforts. This is another way to obtain benchmarks to measure your progress. You probably need to "go dark" in some if not all media to accurately baseline, and not all marketers are willing to do that. Gary urges that all media be "tightly baselined" so as to show the additional traffic driven by the media effort. Darkness is easier to do in pay-per-click advertising than TV and radio, of course. A way to avoid going dark nationally is to "rotate the darkness" in different geographic locales as identified by designated market areas, or DMAs. Most web analytic solutions allow you to identify traffic by DMA and by storing user DMA and treating it as a variable you can get robust reporting on visit geography.

Using this method you may need to go dark (locally) for a longer period to get volume. You can't go dark for too long, of course (a month is ideal), and while you want similar periods of time to measure, you need to avoid using the same times during the year. Gary points out that it's important not to just measure the volume of traffic, but also the quality of traffic.

No matter what online metrics system you are using, audiences may not be who they seem. For example, Gary mentioned that efforts to track "lifetime customer value" on the web are hampered by the phenomena of cookie deletion. To overcome this, Gary suggests "key joining"—joining the cookie data (usually only available for two to six months because of the deletion issue) to other identifiers, such as e-mail addresses. He suggests marketers try aggressively to secure e-mail addresses so as to be able to utilize the cookie data over longer time spans. Gary also advocates doing behavioral segmentation (based on all web behavior and media touch points) and flowing that into the brand's CRM system. Such "microsegmentation" is one of the most powerful ways marketers can use analytics.

Semphonic's vendor-neutral methodology aims for content measurement. Their tactical approach to web analytics focuses on *web pages* as the core unit. This kind of testing can be extremely important in cases where you can see you're getting a lot of traffic into a website, but still not getting the level of response or conversions you are hoping for.

The core idea is that different pages have different functions and that to measure page success you have to measure by function and you can only compare pages within the same function. It makes no sense, for example, to compare a page whose function is to route a user to what they are interested in with a page whose function it is to convince them to buy a product.

Gary also mentioned that Semphonic carves up content into separate buckets they call Informers, Convincers, Re-Assurers, Converters, etc. If you read Chapter 4's material on building a sales funnel, you can easily see where these functions might fit along your funnel, and what kinds of content they might be. For example, Informer content might be a product description; Convincing content might be an industry award or it could be an attractive price; Re-Assuring content might be found in a link to a customer review page. Converting content would remove all further obstacles to a sale—an explanation of easy shipping options, a familiar-looking shopping cart, or the promise of a future discount with purchase.

Bob asked Gary if this was similar to a frame of reference we've written about in which audience cohorts are thought of as "skeptics, agnostics, believers, and evangelists" (in terms of their likelihood to socially promote a brand or product).

"Not quite," Gary said. "That type of audience segmentation is often fundamental and valuable but it isn't quite what I was getting at. This type of functional analysis is very useful for content measurement but it is only half the story. Your type of segmentation is the other half since you should usually be answering a question like 'Is this page working well for Segment X?' not just 'Is this page working well?' Combining the two approaches potentially gives you that answer."

News for Nonprofits: Don't Ignore Global Search!

Pssst! Want to supercharge your search results and lower your cost-per-click? Sure, we all do. Andreas Ramos of Creative Consultants Group (now with Axciom) did just that for the Massachusetts Institute of Technology's OpenCourseWare project, which offers free web classes in thirty-five academic subjects taught at MIT, including basic courses in biology, physics, economics, literature, women's studies, and theatre arts. A wonderful resource, more than 1,600 self-paced classes are offered entirely for free, and can be downloaded as course materials to teachers worldwide.

To help spread the word, MIT received a $450,000 Google Foundation Grant, and Ramos's team was asked to manage the Adwords account that went with it. From an initial dribble of 52 clicks per day, within a month the site's Adwords placements began bringing in up to 17,650 clicks per day, driving down the cost-per-click from $.076 down to $0.07, and increasing the click-through rate from 0.12 percent to 4.02 percent.

How was it done? Google had set up the initial account with 1,400 keywords. To cover all the subjects and classes, Ramos's team added 48,548 more keywords. More importantly, the main keywords were translated into Chinese, Japanese, Korean, German, French, Spanish, Italian, Portuguese, Russian, and Arabic. This despite the fact that only a small percentage of the courseware was translated from English, and then only in Spanish, Portuguese, and Chinese. Throughout the project, the group created multiple ads for each academic subject area, targeted ads to specific subject area landing pages, and used A/B split testing to identify which ads were pulling the best.

Hunger for useful information is global, and in the academic world, English may be the language of schooling but not the native language of the majority. Ramos and his partner, Stephanie Cota, offer these insights, which should resonate with for-profit organizations as well as nonprofit and governmental entities:

- ► Global advertising campaigns are feasible and affordable with channels such as Adwords. In their project, the top 100 best performing keywords were in English, Chinese, Arabic, German, French, and Spanish. Click-through rates for Arabic keywords averaged 30 percent.

- ► Keywords in German attracted online students from around the world, as many German universities are renowned for their science and attract a global student base.

- ► When tracking search results in a global campaign, adjust for local conventions. This doesn't merely mean adjusting for time zones; the workweek in much of the Arab world is from Saturday through Wednesday, for example, and state holidays in some parts of Asia may mean businesses and schools shut down for several days.

SPECIAL SECTION A

Measuring with Marshall

Marshall Sponder is a frequent speaker on social media and its applications to ROI. Currently writing for *Entrepreneur* magazine and his own well-researched blog (www.webmetricsguru.com), he has specialized in search engine optimization (SEO) and web analytics for IBM, Monster.com, and as a consultant and independent contractor to corporations, small businesses, and entrepreneurs on marketing analytics, on issues from isolating the right questions to SEO and campaign evaluation. Here are a few of Marshall's recent tips on using free or inexpensive web tools to optimize your online marketing:

Idea #1: Use Google Analytics to Optimize Your Website

When Google Analytics added benchmarking, this allowed site owners to compare their own sites to others in the same category (see Figure 6-10). Of course, many sites fit into more than one category, and to enable benchmarking, you must first enable data sharing from within your analytics settings. Using my art blog, ArtNewYorkCity.com, I wanted to see how well it performs against other blogs in its category.

Selecting the right category is crucial for this exercise—fortunately, Google Analytics has a fairly rich selection to choose from, especially if you drill down a few levels.

Once you have chosen a category, you can view up to six charts comparing your site with the averages of other sites in its category, aggregated from several thousand sites using Google Analytics that have also elected to share their data with the world (the data is stripped of any personal information).

While my site gets exactly the average amount of visits of a typical art website, according to Google Analytics, it's by far above average in its very low bounce rate—according to the top right chart, the typical art site has a bounce rate of approximately 51 percent, while mine hovers between the 3%–5% range—and that's a question to explore.

Figure 6-10. Comparisons to benchmarks.

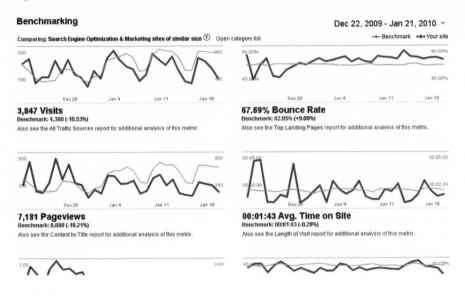

However, the average art site has a significantly longer visit than mine, 2 minutes and 20 seconds on average, while an Art-NewYorkCity.com visit lasts 1 minute and 20 seconds (which would seem long enough—but comparing it to other sites leads me to think about improvements I should make to encourage my readers to stay on the site longer).

On the other hand, while the typical art website gets three pages per visit, ArtNewYorkCity.com gets seven pages per visit—a phenomenal number, all things being considered (it's a blog, and that means the typical visitor looks at seven of my posts on an average visit).

Almost all the visits to ArtNewYorkCity.com are from new visitors, yet the average art blog has about 70% of its traffic from new visitors. That might be a good thing—it shows there is a loyal group or community that revisits some sites more often than others. I'd rather have half my visitors be repeat than all of them be new.

Taking a step back, it's easy to take this information, look at your site, and start to brainstorm ideas and suggestions that would improve it. It's a good idea to figure out steps you can take to improve your site, according to what you find in Google Analytics, and then use benchmarking again after a few days to see if your ideas are working or not.

If you don't succeed right away, keep at it. Sooner or later, by using Google Analytics Benchmarking, your site will improve, and you'll be able to see it via the benchmarks—just remember to always compare your site to the same category you started off with.

Idea #2: Find Influentials in the Twitter Stream

Here's an example of how to find influential social media analytics individuals—but of course, it'll work only to the extent an individual's Twitter profile has that information in it (and if we get to the point where Semantic Analysis will fill that information in, even if it's not entered anywhere in the profile—and it's accurate—we'll have something even better)!

1. Go to www.TweepSearch.com and enter "social media analyst." See Figure 6-11.
2. Use Excel Web Query to pull the entire page into Excel (will work with 2003 or 2007 versions). Notice that I checked the entire page in the upper right—pull in everything. See Figure 6-12.

Figure 6-11. Result of TweepSearch query.

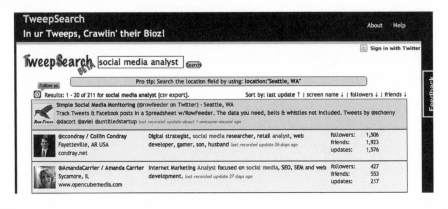

Figure 6-12. Closeup of web query screen shot.

3. Press "Import." The entire page is imported minus any pictures. You can guess the rest. You can collect all 14 pages of data, paste it on the same page, then do some formatting magic (which I won't go into here), and collect the data into a nice, neat table.

Let's step back and talk about why I found influentials this way. Why didn't I use Radian6 or Sysomos or Alterian/Techrigy/SM2? I have access to all of them—and I use them a lot—and I tried Sysomos Map, and got some good stuff—but what I pulled from TweepSearch was actually better than anything I could get from any of the platforms above.

Here's why:

What people "say" when they speak, or when they write, isn't often an accurate description of "who they are." Radian6, Sysomos, Alterian/Techrigy/SM2, and almost all the platforms for Social Media Monitoring work by canvassing the stream of conversations—but that doesn't tell us who they are so we can decide if we want to contact them or not.

What a person puts in their Twitter Profile may or may not be accurate, but at least it's a self-identified deceleration of what they say they do, what they say they believe—and it's much easier to work with that than work with the "overall conversations."

It also makes me think I should update my own Twitter Profile to better reflect what I really do—and maybe you should too.

Idea #3: Measure Mobile Advertising with Bar Codes

When I read a post [in MobiADNews] stating "Google Puts QR Codes On 100,000 Stores," I got an intuitive flash, that QR

Codes—[what we call bar codes]—could be the missing link to social media monitoring attribution, the one we've been looking for:

> ... In a move to link online content to real world locations, **Google** has launched a new QR-code based **Favorite Places on Google** program.
>
> Google has identified the top 100,000 most searched stores in the US, and has sent them a window decal that includes a unique QR code. When consumers scan the code with their phone, they go directly to a Google mobile web **Place Page** about the business.
>
> ... After a company is registered in the LBC, Google identifies the most popular by keeping track of how often consumers search for that business, how often they ask for directions, etc.
>
> Periodically Google will send out an additional wave of window decals to a new set of "most popular" businesses. There is no way for a company to request such a decal, it has to be earned though consumer interaction.
>
> Consumers can then interact with the Place Page in various ways. For example, they can read reviews to see what other users think about the business, they can find any coupons that the business may be offering, or they can leave their own review of the business.

When I first read that I immediately saw its potential to link back to the Social Media ROI, the part everyone wants to have using that QR code. I've maintained for years that technology isn't really an issue, the means exist to track just about anything you want, now, in full Technicolor details, including cross-channel conversions, and even engagement.

If it's possible to track Social Media ROI, why haven't we?

Because it's hard. You have to agree with what you want to

measure and set up your tracking for every possible circumstance ahead of time—and who is willing to do that? Most people aren't aware of all the things it's possible to track, much less how to track them using Analytics.

With the QR codes linked into the Local Business Center—where you can also add a lot of your business information and list coupons—you now have a way of tracking Social Media, if you want to think strategically.

I also think Google should let every business listed generate it's own QR code and link it into Google Analytics, as it appears to be doing for the 100,000 businesses it has already generated codes and decals for. See Figure 6-13.

The issue isn't really reading the QR Codes, as most mobile phones are capable, with the right software, of doing so. Since Mobile Phone adoption is so widespread, it seems likely that Social Media ROI will be plugged into Mobile Phone and Mobile Application growth—meaning that the two will converge and have been with applications like FourSquare [a geocentric social media site that sells advertising. With the proliferation of free barcode reading apps most phones could be fitted with barcode readers, and users would receive incentives, such as the badges given by FourSquare, to use them often].

So how would it work? How could you take a brick-and-mortar business, say a local restaurant chain, and turn it on to Social Media ROI using Google's Local Business Center and QR codes?

A local restaurant (the example shown in Google's product introduction video) can list menu items, hours, and coupons (all which are tracked by built-in Google Analytics, based on what I'm seeing in the video). Since Google is now including Twitter's real-time feed into Google's Search Results and is trying to do

Figure 6-13. QR codes and Google Analytics.

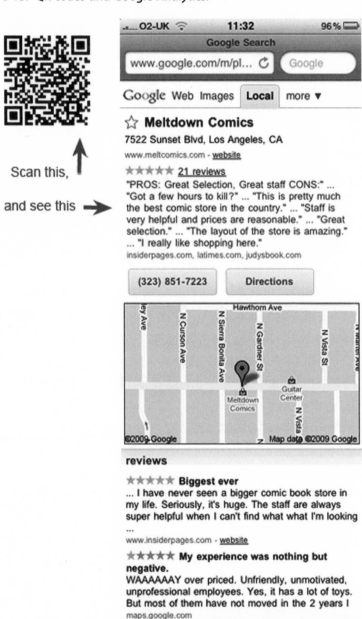

Scan this,

and see this ➡

the same with Facebook (to the extent that privacy settings allow for updates to be published), the analytics in Google's Local Business Center should be able to correlate community advocacy with social media activity driven by it.

When the customer prints out a coupon from Google Local Business Center . . . or . . . shows up at the restaurant for a meal . . . and uses the QR Scanner on . . . say, the menu items, or a special offer . . . they will be tied in directly to the promotional efforts and ROI from the Social Media activities will be established.

All we needed, then, was a way of working, of conceptualizing how to tie Social Media and the enabling technology to tie in the actual act of taking part in Social Media—of being influenced to show up and try a meal—all of that, I think, can be tracked using the QR codes. Now, that doesn't mean most businesses are doing that now—they aren't—but they could. The answer is not technology by itself, but strategic thinking and technology together.

Right now, we need to go and try it—let's see what happens when we think up a program we want to track and get the pieces in place. While Google doesn't generate the QR codes for 99.9 percent of the businesses that need them, you can still generate QR codes easily on your own with QR generators from companies such as QR Stuff (www.qrstuff.com), which sells a scanner as an iPhone app, sets up codes, and will even print them on a T-shirt.

CHAPTER 7

ROI in the Enterprise

WHY BUILD A ROI CULTURE in your department, or in your company? The best answer is that best-in-class companies are those that keep their eye on the bottom line, and those that have always kept a sharper eye on incremental income opportunities and a tight lid on expense leaks.

Marketers are in a great age of transition. The media channels we are familiar with are disappearing from the world (newspapers, local radio, analog TV) and with them, the ways we measured success. In fact, it's getting harder to find folks who remember how to measure them—newcomers to the field have never seen a Bacon's media directory or paged through an *SRDS* reference guide.

In their place are a new breed of marketers who dizzy themselves with the latest news or tools from marketing blogs, and scores of analysts who can produce reams of web metrics and are still confusing soft data with ROI data.

In the confusion, you're going to see your agency friends and public relations gurus attempting to sell you old-fashioned CPMs on new-fashioned media. Your ad server partners and IT suppliers will be hawking bidding tools that give you a microsecond edge over competitors online, and glaze your eyes with PowerPoint presentations and demo videos as to how these expenditures are really an investment in your organization.

If you've read this far, you now have some idea of how to measure the return on your marketing investments, whether they are the free balloons with your phone number on it that you give out at a street fair, or the million-dollar ad spend on a combined TV, web, and mobile campaign. This chapter will help you put together what you know so you can present it to senior management. And it can help you make the case for changes in the organization that can put all departments on the same track. We'll also talk a bit about how to create ROI protocols in companies that are not sales-driven. This is important to nonprofits and schools. It is increasingly used in government media, as state, federal, and local budgets have shrunk in recent years.

Case in Point: A Social Network Campaign at Hardin-Simmons

At Hardin-Simmons University, whenever we did fundraising mailings, at the end of the day, we looked at how much money we raised per dollar spent. It's a solid metric to see if what we're doing was working or not.

We also were able to demonstrate real value from our social network campaigns. Here's one example:

In 2007, HSU was approached by the local NBC affiliate, KRBC-

TV, about an advertising and promotion opportunity. After several meetings between the HSU marketing and recruiting groups and station management, we were able to create a truly win/win scenario. HSU wanted to do more than just advertise on the station; we wanted the station to have "skin in the game" to increase our opportunity to make an impact on the recruiting goals for the university. The station wanted to extend its reach and create an event that could drive viewers in the all-important May sweeps rating period. The solution was "Lights, Camera, Free Ride."

The concept was fairly simple: prospective students would send in a one- to two-minute video about why they were right for HSU, or what they would do with their diploma from HSU. Videos would be aired during the 6:00 P.M. and 10:00 P.M. newscasts on KRBC. At the end of the promotion, a winning video would be selected and that student would receive a full tuition waiver for his or her freshman year. Since HSU is a private university, this equated to a "prize" worth more than $20,000.

HSU also created an award-winning thirty-second commercial entitled "My Diploma" with lyrics sung to the tune of The Knack's classic punk rock hit, "My Sharona." *M-m-m-my Diploma* is still ringing in the ears of viewers. See Figure 7-1 on page 196.

The goal was to create a lyric that would stick in viewers' minds; we wanted to get people talking about HSU. This seemed to work as letters were written to the local newspaper asking who created the commercial and how it was done. This extra coverage created additional advertising equivalency value that could bejewel the ROI crown.

HSU invested $2,250 during the 2009 campaign for the commercial to air during shows like *The Office* and others known to be popular among high school students on KRBC and its corporate sister station, KTAB-TV. Production of the commercial was done in-house at no cost by HSU's gifted videographer and webmaster, Robert Erin Leeper, utilizing Flash animated text to drive the words home and capture viewer attention. Vocal Trash, a popular touring band led by HSU alumnus Steve Linder, recorded the jingle. The group donated their recording time to the university and received a letter for tax purposes.

In 2007 and 2008, postcards were sent out to prospective students encouraging them to enter and directing them to a website for contest details. Printing and mailing the postcards cost about $1,500. Recruiters sent e-mails to their cadres of prospects. Online guerilla marketing was employed by HSU's marketing office, with student interns seeding the web with discussions about the contest. As MySpace and Facebook usage exploded during this time, the online marketing efforts morphed almost completely into Facebook marketing, eliminating the production and mailing costs of the announcement postcard in 2009. Instead, a fan page for the promotion was created and a targeted Facebook Ads cost-per-click campaign was undertaken at a cost of about $500 to drive prospects to the fan page and the details page on the HSU website.

KRBC produced and ran a commercial for "Lights, Camera, Free Ride" to encourage students to enter and see their video on the newscasts. As part of their commitment, KRBC also ran between five and ten news stories about HSU each week during the promotional period. These additional mentions of HSU helped to enhance an already substantial mountain of advertising equivalency value. At a conservative average of $350 per thirty-second spot, HSU received more than 150 segments of equivalent time. (This does not include the time for the entire 5:00 P.M. and 6:00 P.M. newscasts aired live from the quad on the HSU campus.) By textbook standards used to estimate the value of commercial airtime, HSU received an equivalent

$52,500 in value from television alone for an investment of less than $3,000. While not applicable to ROI calculations, this was an impressive soft metric in PR terms.

The positive impressions created among high school students and the community were also not directly measurable. The buzz online, although substantial, did not reliably translate into a countable metric.

What *could* be counted was the number of potential students who submitted a video and later went on to apply to the University. Given the unusually small expense of the campaign (approximately $25,000, which included the contest prize of tuition), even a single matriculating student would make the campaign approach the break-even point between marketing expense and revenue. We could also look at the number of video submissions and applications from potential students within the TV station's geographic market area, and compare them to applicants from outside the area who might have been exposed only to the postcard and/or social media outreach.

While hardly on the scale of a national brand contest, the results were gratifying. Just forty-two prospective students entered a video, but of these, forty became first-year students at HSU! When the revenue from their tuition is figured into the ROI equation, the ROI percentage hovers at 3,000 percent. We mention this example because it was a branding initiative that had trackable elements common to many other campaigns: mailing lists, contest promotion, a clear call to action that helped qualify the best prospects, and a solid revenue goal. The branding elements were also pretty common: TV advertising, public relations, viral seeding. Unlike many branding campaigns, however, it had a solid revenue goal as its bottom line and made the most of its small budget.

One thing we don't know is how many students would have come anyway. Participating students often used their friends and family to

Figure 7-1. Applicant-produced YouTube video for "My Diploma."

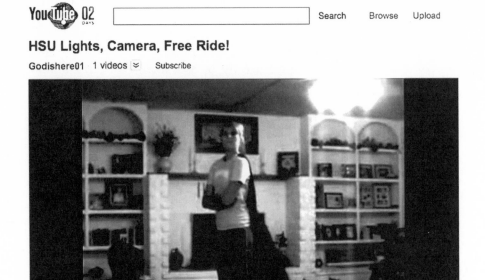

help them with their videos, so there was a "passalong" benefit that could not be calculated, yet may have long-term benefits to the brand.

Obstacles to Becoming a Metrics–Driven Marketer

Contrary to what you may think, it's not your budget that's holding back your organization. If all you can afford is Google Analytics (free) and your competition is paying for everything Nielsen and Omniture can sell, you can still use the metrics, tap your creativity, and deploy your knowledge of ROI to succeed.

Organizational structure is usually what keeps a marketer down. Through this book, we've talked about creating documents that all stakeholders can view and understand. You can take those same documents and streamline them to present upwards as well.

What Do They Want to Know?

Everybody's heard the story of the marketing analyst who prepares a thirty-minute slide show or forty-page document for a meeting with top brass, only to be asked a single question: "How much money did we make?" Truly this is the question, especially if the second one is "And you spent how much to do this?"

Executives always want to know how actions affect the bottom line. They're somewhat myopic that way. But look at all of your channels, and see how you can break it down. You can break it down by campaign initiative, but it makes a simpler presentation if you break it down by media channel: e-mail, direct mail, print ads, website, etc.

Here's a six-step battle plan for presenting the results of your media campaign:

Step #1: *List each channel, and assign a "sales generated" unit or dollar number to it.* This may be overly simplistic, and that dreaded "overhead" problem may present itself, but with some experimentation, you can determine formulas and weighting factors to make each number plausible.

Grouping Internet spending for presentation, as a complete online channel (in the way that print ads are) can help you avoid the pitfalls of line-item pruning and simplistic assumptions.

The risk is that someone will see that search is delivering a far better dollar-for-dollar-spent return, and start pulling down the branding channels to save money. As we discussed in our previous book, *Digital Engagement*, when others tried this, they found that their search numbers suffered. There are still marketers out there comparing all Internet sales results to those trackable by search, even though we know now that banners and social media affect search metrics and purchase behaviors.

Step #2: *Frame the discussion with specifics.* You'll get these from your goals you set out (see Chapter 5) and should not be afraid to get specific.

"Our goal was to increase the number of qualified sales leads by 10 percent, and sales by 3 percent, during this quarter" is better than saying, "Our goal was to increase our qualified sales leads." Now it may be the fact that you were aiming for 25 percent increase in leads, and like the character Scotty in the old TV series *Star Trek*, were building in a cushion to look like a hero even if your own expectations were not met. And you may have set a deadline in your mind (nine months) that's different from the time frame on your spreadsheet (three months). This in fact might allow you to analyze long-term effects of a branding program, even if management only wants to see short-term results. In the C-suite, be specific in dollars, units, percentages, and time frame. You'll be better understood by all.

And it is also quite possible that the top executives don't want to hear your results presented in ROI terms at all. Our friend Andreas Ramos at Acxiom is an old hand when it comes to six-figure search budgets, and he says the toughest executives always want to see and compare revenue numbers, not ROI.

"ROI is not an objective number," says Ramos. "ROI is a political number. I've interviewed many CFOs and directors of finance. They don't use ROI. They use complex models that are based on company strategy, i.e., internal politics. I used to think that CFOs were objective and neutral. They're actually intensely political."

Thus to the eagle-eyed exec you will be prepared to present the true *net revenue* numbers in your equations. That is, the sold price of the product or service, minus what it cost to produce it. As a marketing person, all the data you may have is gross revenues or gross sales. If you've been using this as your net revenue number, you may be expected or asked to also run the equation with *gross margin* or *gross profit* numbers. Or the CFO may also inquire about the *contribution margin*, or CM. These are all interchangeable terms for *net revenue*; again, it is the sold price of the product or service minus the cost to produce it. (We advise checking with your accounting department for definitions to make sure you are indeed speaking the same language within your organization.) While as a marketing person you have no control over production costs, and perhaps only slight control over the selling price, you should try to obtain the gross revenue or CM of product categories if you are talking about a specific product, such as a recent launch of a new line.

Generally you will be safe if you aggregate gross revenues if it's established that this indeed is all you are personally responsible for. But Ramos cautions: "There's another problem with ROI: it works only for similar products in similar sizes. You can't use it as a metric of profitability across various industries or different products. It doesn't scale and it doesn't transfer. The ROI on a lemonade stand can't compare with the ROI of Intel." In other words, comparing the return of coupon redemption between an established product and a new product could seriously backfire, and kill not only the new product marketing budget but the new product as well.

Step #3: *Address the issue most affecting the organization at the time of your presentation.* This is sometimes referred to as "speaking to the pain." Find your company's pain point—it might be low sales in a certain territory, or embarrassment over higher Google rankings by small-time competitors, or a bad public relations event they'd love to paper over before the stockholders hear of it.

Step #4: *Don't just present results, present the action plan you've created from viewing the results.* In fact, in some organizations, it's better to pitch the action plan if you're short on face time, and just use the ROI results to back up your case for your proposals.

Step #5: *Make sure your numbers are accurate.* Double-check figures or have someone look them over for you. Make friends with someone in finance if this is your weak point.

Step #6: *Make the presentations in person wherever you can.* Sending in weekly reports by e-mail, or worse, forwarding automated reports generated by your agency or web server, practically guarantees they won't get read. You should be able to summarize your report in thirty seconds of speech (practice!) and have available a one-page handout that clearly shows your action plan and the relevant numbers. Adding a finalized ROI equation for the initiative rarely fails to impress. Those are the numbers that count: *marketing investment, net revenues,* and the resulting ROI percentage that meets or beats its hurdle rate.

Dashboard or Excel File?

You don't have to work in web media to get the benefit of a dashboard. Even brick-and-mortar stores use them to track both revenue and expenses. This can become a useful tool for all stakeholders, as well as for top brass.

Eastern Mountain Sports, the sport clothing retailer, created its own dashboard system in-house that allowed product managers to view individual stores sales for the products in their line. One shoe product manager noticed a spike in not just shoe sales but all sales at just one of seventy-five retail outlets. A visit to the store revealed that the spike could be attributed to a single employee, later dubbed "the shoe guru," who had trained himself to fit customers perfectly and to knowledgeably answer all their questions about all the sport shoes sold in the store. Today, every EMS store has its own "shoe guru"—a trained employee to sell shoes and upsell appropriate accessories, such as specially padded socks for hiking or skiing.

Dashboards have grown in popularity as more organizations want to look at their data in real time. If you're a do-it-yourselfer, you can generate visual dashboards from your own Excel files, using tutorials on the web from Pointy Haired Dilbert (http://chandoo.org/wp/2008/08/20/create-kpi-dashboards-excel-1/) or from Microsoft, or template purveyors (http://www.anychart.com/products/anychart/docs/users-guide/dashboard-creation-tutorial.html). The website Dashboard Spy (www.dashboardspy.com) usually has the most up-to-date developments, and always has a plethora of guest-submitted dashboards to show what's new.

Google Analytics, of course, will generate dashboards for your web efforts, and most web analytics programs now include plug-ins that assist imports of data into various spreadsheets, including Excel. There are small software vendors out there, such as Shufflepoint (http://www.shufflepoint.com/ExcelWebQuery.aspx), that will allow you to convert Google into Excel if that is the preferred presentation format in your company.

All the metrics of your marketing investments, and the revenues they affect, should be illustrated in media that can be viewed or transmitted electronically, even if you are asked to prepare hard copy reports.

Keep the conversion funnel in mind as well as your key indicators. Here's another quick-and-dirty four-column trick to match up social media mentions and sales:

First column: results from a social media measurement platform, or direct from site side data that shows click-throughs to your website.

Second column: resulting numbers of new visitors, if you are separating them from your existing customer base. Theoretically, if your marketing efforts in social media have been successful, these visitors should have a higher degree of conversions than existing customers or those arriving from other points on the web.

Third column: this holds sales data (or other conversion data) matched to the visitors.

Fourth column: comparative percentage of conversions, as compared to that of existing customers or a benchmark of your choosing. Assuming you have input the *marketing investment* for the social media program and *net revenues* accurately, you should be able to compare the ROI of your social media program to other forms of outreach.

If your situation suggests that clear graphics and charts will get your point across better, take another look at the sales funnel and dashboard examples in Chapter 4.

Adjusting ROI Factors in Your Favor

This is our favorite part, and it's the hardest to do, even if you are the boss of the company. Sometimes your ROI results will indicate that resources and even departments would be best rearranged to get the most profit for your marketing dollars. If you are the marketing manager, your ROI investigations may have uncovered operations from other departments that weaken, damage, or just plain sabotage your ROI. Common errors typically come from customer service (orders are delayed before being fulfilled, which means your revenues are delayed another thirty or sixty days); from inventory gaps (factory failed to ship product featured in a special promotion); or from support staff (mailroom or printer failed to bulk-mail catalogs, IT took a week off instead of fixing the glitch on your shopping cart interface). Having proof (such as the ROI spreadsheet shown in Figure 2-1) of other factors that affected your ROI can help affect change.

Here are a few strategies to bring to the C-Suite for review:

Strategy #1: **Redefine Marketing Teams**   Create a new one on the fly. Just try it! Include IT, sales, PR, customer service, and, where applicable, finance, R&D, and production. In a large organization these kinds of roundtables tend to be stiff, formal, and regularly scheduled—and often vague to the point of meaninglessness. See about getting a small group together to discuss a specific initiative. If you're a small organization, try to pull everyone together for coffee, and include your outside vendors for public relations and tech support, and present your planned campaign to them. Invite all stakeholders and be prepared for useful criticism. Retool with suggestions before launch (or lunch).

Strategy #2: **Get Rid of Silos**   Ephraim Cohen, a principal of The Fortex Group and Edelman alumnus, had some good pointers in a recent article for the IABC (International Association of Business Communicators). He suggests extending branding or PR programs to include sales staff. This can be anything from bringing sales personnel to a product launch, to making copies of media placements for distribution by salespeople. He goes on to elaborate: "For example, media relations programs can be extended to include the creation and distribution of reprints to prospects. Reprints of articles can be far more effective in pushing along the sales prospects, as this is some of the strongest third-party literature available."

The only thing we, as web marketers, would add to Cohen's recommendations is to suggest that you make a webcast of the CEO's presentation or send along a link of the media placement with the suggestion that sales teams forward these as e-mails to their prospects.

In the most successful organizations, sales staffers have lunch with marketing staffers all the time. If you're having trouble getting numbers for your *net revenues* calculation, befriend the sales crew or pay them a formal call and ask for help. They've got the numbers, and you've both got a common mission: to sell more. Nobody knows why the western territory doesn't sell enough Fritos or Frisbees better than the staff of the western sales team.

One obstacle you may find is that the sales team is far removed, or may not exist within the employee realm at all. In 2010, book publisher Simon & Schuster, which sells trade hardcovers and paperbacks to bookstores large and small, fired thirty of its regional salespeople and replaced them with a centralized call center. Customer service and fulfillment are often also done by an outsourced call center. Yours may be in another state, or in another country. If this is the case, the executive in charge of hiring the call center is probably getting reports that may yield useful CRM data. Ask—it never hurts to ask— for some recent "samples" of the report. Say you're investigating a cost-cutting API (which in fact you are).

Dissolving the wall with the IT staff is easier than it looks, because odds are good your web analytics staff and your IT team would really love to get involved in marketing decisions. After all, they've been saying how they could do your job so much better—behind your back we hope. To wit:

> If you are an Executive, invite an Analyst to a meeting as an observer. Have the Analyst sit in the back of the room, and don't let the Analyst speak unless spoken to. Let the Analyst hear real business issues, and let the Analyst listen to the interactions that happen as decisions are actually made. There's no more valuable thing for an Analyst than to see how things actually work, so that the Analyst can calibrate work in a way that makes the Analyst more effective.—*Mindthatdata.com (Kevin Hillstrom)*

We also endorse the notion of making friends with finance. Asking someone to look over a spreadsheet with ROI for a minor initiative is one way to test the waters and can be helpful if you're not handy with Excel.

Strategy #3: **Take Analytics Back into the Marketing Department** Current theory suggests that marketing may be the bridge IT has been looking for, as its own entry into the executive suite. We've seen industry blogs suggesting that analytics staffers cultivate colleagues in the marketing department.

Having web analytics at arm's length is a holdover from the days of pricey mainframe computers that cost millions to run. Today's entrepreneurs can look at their server-side metrics on the patios of their vacation homes, using Google Analytics. Why should a corporate marketing executive have to get the same data from a human intermediary?

If you can't get password access, ask questions repeatedly until it's less bother to just give you password access. Study a few basics first.

Download informational videos and PDFs and learn how to read a site report.

This is the basic information you should get from IT:

▶ Web traffic, defined as visitors, unique visitors, repeat visitors.

▶ Completed actions and non-completed actions that help you identify leads. Can you compare page views of your site registration page with actual registrations? Can you see how many times shopping carts are abandoned? What is the bounce rate (visitors leaving before taking action) and which pages are responsible for most bounce and may need to be tweaked?

▶ Time spent on site. This is useful if you have an informational site. For nonprofits, this may be an important metric. Commercial sites will vary, depending on the complexity of the purchase, and are not always any predictor of actual sales.

▶ Sales data where available. One of the most irritating aspects of a ROI exercise is that sales data generated from an e-commerce database may not agree with another database in use by your automated sales force system. Run a few sample tests to discover if a variance is regular enough to create an offset number that will correlate both sets of data with only a modest degree of inaccuracy.

Do not take any single set of numbers on faith. Most enterprises that use web metrics reporting systems usually run a second system (Google Analytics or something else that is free) as a backup. While standardization among reporting systems has improved significantly in the last couple of years, two or three different counting systems will usually yield two or three different results.

Strategy #4. **Realign the PR Department**   All branding initiatives should answer to marketing, even if control of some branding campaigns is across the hall in the public relations department. Beware of new media power grabs. And resource poaching: a recent survey from *PR Week* found that 48 percent of those responding (i.e., public relations executives) planned to fund social media campaigns with dollars from the marketing budget, while only 18 percent planned to use the PR budget for this new area of spending.

For your part, we suggest you do your best to dump legacy promotional spending into the public relations budget, not the marketing budget. You may also wish to move social media spending under the PR umbrella also, if you have not yet perfected a sales or conversion funnel that matches social media to revenue.

If you'd like to keep such line items under your budgetary control, do ROI calculations on their effectiveness. Then separate them out in presentations to make the case for decreasing or increasing marketing spend in those areas.

If social media is already in the hands of outsourced PR professionals, the webmaster, or the IT department, align those initiatives with what you're spending on search, and combine them into a single channel that can be broken out for analysis as needed. If you are already skilled in multi-channel web marketing and have faith in your outsourced experts, consider putting together an Excel-based ROI grid that all participants can view and understand.

Strategy #5: **Make Customer Service and CRM Systems Pull Their Weight**   Customer service is usually the missing link between a successful marketing campaign and a successful sale. It doesn't matter how fabulous your advertising campaign is, if a customer gets a rude welcome at the cash register, you're going to lose the sale. *And* the customer will probably complain to high heaven (or at least to Twitter and Facebook) about how much they hate your brand.

You probably see CRM and CSM data or can access this data if you want. Lowered revenues may be caused by delayed shipping, delayed billing, returns, or rebates sent to customers, either as a bounty or as a consolation prize for bad service. Since returns are a debit on the *net revenues* side of the equation, always question anomalies and use your gut instinct as well as your common sense. Weather is often a factor in brick-and-mortar enterprises; human error is usually the bigger one.

A nexus of customer service with social media is the "listening" service that monitors the web for positive and negative brand mentions. This is often outsourced and comes in two flavors: companies that automate "sentiment analysis" by recording key terms and even emoticons, and companies that use human monitors for at least some part of the survey of the webstream. Smaller companies can use Google Alert, which feeds a continuous stream of mentions to any e-mail account. Best-in-class companies like IBM and American Express do their own monitoring of social media, alert to issues that may affect brand perceptions among customers. These two companies, among others, also monitor the social media used by their employees, and so does the American Red Cross with its volunteers.

Strategy #6: **Get Out from Under Your Overhead** In Chapter 2 and in the Special Section on ROI Basics, we've tried to make the case that overhead charges do not need to be applied to the *net revenues* part of your marketing ROI equations, and they should never be an additional dollar factor on your *marketing investment* side. If you can't convince the finance department to remove overhead charges from your dollar factors, always separate them out in presentations. Do

ROI calculations with and then without overhead and present your findings. You may be able to adjust the percentage of overhead allotted to your department, or argue for more resources, if it's clear you are contributing in large measure.

Not Sales Driven? You Still Need ROI

Not long ago we met a young professional in charge of branding initiatives for a large Midwestern insurance company. The operation had a budget of just under seven figures, much of it used to underwrite sponsorships of college football. While these marketing investments had to be accounted for, there was no pressure to link the dollars spent to gaining new insurance customers, and no measures in place to try to see if branding sports events was a legacy loser or a lead generator. We wonder if that's still true, because even nonprofits are being held to accountability for every dime they spend.

Several nonprofits report increases in fundraising from social media outreach programs that involve photography that's variously inspirational or heartrending. The Humane Society of the United States tracked over $650,000 in donations from a single online photo contest on Flickr, a photo-sharing site. Emboldened, it moved on to a campaign to persuade the International House of Pancakes restaurant chain to use cage-free eggs, enlisting 17,000 Twitter followers, and an informational campaign on its pages at MySpace, Facebook, and YouTube (as of this writing, IHOP has yet to bend).

Small nonprofits can take heart from Epic Change (Case Study #4), which raised $11,000 in forty-eight hours on Twitter to build a classroom in Tanzania. Over 98 percent of the donors had never donated to Epic Change previously, which proves that social media is not only trackable, it is a cost-effective means to extend a brand that can spur people to action if the message hits home. Epic Change is a very small nonprofit, and has been generous with its metrics to show other nonprofits how to track ROI and return responsible accounting to their donors and friends.

The Future of Trackable Marketing

The impetus to track every single dollar of a marketing spend and make it accountable to ROI is equally matched by roiling changes in the way advertising is being sold to marketers through every sort of channel. In the same way that bidding for Internet search terms has become an arcane science of numbers and incremental fractions of a cent, marketers may soon find themselves having to bid up their competitors to obtain access to audiences as auction-based advertising exchanges move from web advertising to print and electronic channels.

When audiences can be fully targeted and profiled, they become more valuable. More specifically, it is the data that becomes more valuable. Ad networks and branded media may become subservient in exchanges to brokers who will buy and sell the customer profiles you have generated to competitors who will pay a higher price for captured names, addresses, and demographics.

There are a few alternatives for marketers to beat the system. The first is to create more personal relationships with customers through social media and vigorously build and maintain your own lists. Web technology has made one-on-one direct marketing to millions an affordable reality for small and large companies alike. As a marketer you should not only own your data, but also understand how to mine it for value and repeat business over time.

The second good strategy is to continue to provide marketing creativity that transcends its initial medium and can be expanded by audience evangelists. It's true, we haven't talked much about creativity in this book, but we all know that the biggest advertising budget doesn't guarantee a creative, compelling message. And shoestring operations can become successes when the marketing message finds that perfect pitch between the prospective customer's needs and the organization's offering.

Targeting isn't everything, either. Gian Fulgoni, chairman of comScore, says marketers should use their ability to track and test messaging ROI *to increase the amount of testing* before a marketing campaign goes out the door. We agree; too often e-mails are sent into the ether without pretesting that could improve conversions by significant amounts; there are too many tote bags being given away with no call to action previously A/B tested for its ability to pull in a sales lead.

ROI measurement isn't just something the marketer can use in the aftermath of a campaign. It can also be effective as a predictive tool. Small tests on messaging or on channels prior to launch may return more than just their cost; they can save you time and energy as well as money.

To quote Fulgioni directly:

No longer can we slap a few alternative banners together, run them in a real-world campaign and measure click rates to gauge the branding impact. The click has been shown to be irrelevant in that regard. No, we need to do our homework before the online campaign runs and make sure we have a persuasive branding message.

The importance of creative was vividly brought home to me more than thirty years ago when, as a young researcher, I was analyzing a TV weight test for a leading beverage company. The company wanted to measure what would happen if it increased TV spending behind one of its major brands by a factor of four.

We used the AdTel split cable ad testing system to deliver the higher weight level to one group of panelists, while keeping the weight steady among a balanced control group. We then compared the brand buying behavior of panelists exposed to the higher TV weight with the behavior of the control group of panelists exposed to the normal weight level. To my surprise, after six months and later after a year of testing, we could see no increase in buying of the advertised brand among those panelists exposed to the heavy weight level.

How could that be, I wondered? Four times the normal TV weight level meant that the company was spending huge amounts of ad money behind the brand—well north of $100 million in today's dollars.

The answer came when we looked at the results of copy tests of the particular TV commercials being used. The research showed that the TV ads were doing a particularly poor job of persuasively communicating a value that would succeed in attracting new buyers or even creating a compelling reason for existing brand buyers to buy more. I'll never forget what the client's wise research manager said to me: "Gian, you need to remember that four times zero is still zero!"

Mathematical laws aren't about to change on our behalf: four times zero will always be zero.

In short order we see that social media is being captured and made trackable to the sales funnel in ways that have only begun to emerge in general usage. But bear in mind that social media are just the latest media to attract marketing dollars, and Twitter and apps may go the way of widgets and MySpace for attention and impact.

One thing that won't change is the need for marketers to continue to move along a path to responsible reporting that makes marketing's contributions clear to decision makers. Creativity can't move forward without organizational support. Harnessing ROI finance principles to your initiatives may not be able to predict your future, but with it, you will always know where you stand.

Epic Change: Small Change Is Fine for a Small Nonprofit

A 2007 volunteer trip to Tanzania inspired San Francisco–based web entrepreneur Sanjay Patel to found Epic Change with Stacy Monk, a graduate of the Heinz School of Public Policy & Management at Carnegie Mellon University who had previously worked with Deloitte Consulting, Genentech, and the Santa Clara Social Services Agency. A few years later, they used their knowledge of the web and Monk's well-honed ROI skills to raise $11,000 in forty-eight hours on Twitter to build a classroom in Tanzania. Says Monk, "Social media represented a way for us to share [our] stories with the broadest possible audience for the lowest possible cost." The result was also a branding success: Over 98 percent of the donors had never donated to Epic Change previously.

Epic Change had multiple goals for social media: they wanted to build connections to reach a broad audience, raise money quickly to achieve their missions, and they wanted to use media that was free.

The campaign was called "Tweetsgiving." Stacy Monk described how it got started:

> TweetsGiving was imagined 6 days before it was launched in response to a very kind thank you post by Avi Kaplan, a volunteer I'd met on Twitter. When I read his blog post, I was moved by his kindness, and wondered what it might be like if, for 2 days, the entire Twitterverse unanimously celebrated gratitude. We started so close to Thanksgiving because of its timeliness during the holiday, because we thought we could sustain momentum for 48 hours, and because we needed the full 6 days from idea to launch to prepare the site and strategy. TweetsGiving raised over $11,000 in 48 hours, almost entirely from the Twitterverse; I did not publicize the effort to previous donors, and only 6 out of 372

contributors had previously donated to Epic Change. TweetsGiving simply wouldn't have been possible without Twitter.

Here's a look at the soft metrics, compiled by Avi Kaplan. In all there were 9,456 visits from 7,563 unique visitors resulting in 15,830 total pageviews. Figure 7-2 shows a basic breakdown of where that traffic came from including the five biggest traffic sources to the site.

A deeper breakdown is as follows:

twitter.com (referral)	3,700	39.13%
(direct) (none)	2,993	31.65%
search (organic)	608	6.43%
facebook.com (referral)	378	4.00%
google.com (referral)	172	1.82%

Figure 7-2. Social media outperformed search engines for the TweetsGiving.

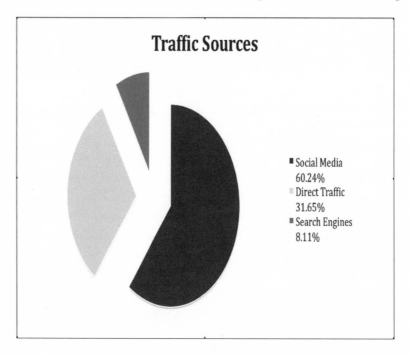

Other statistics compiled and shared:

▶ Over 3,000 gratitude tweets posted that included the TweetsGiving hash tag.

▶ TweetsGiving was one of the top trending terms over the forty-eight hours of the campaign.

▶ $11,021 was raised in 364 donations tracked from the site's donation page, which included options such as Googlepay, Paypal, and a downloadable form for use with mailed checks.

▶ The TweetsGiving site had 15,830 total page views from 7,563 unique visitors in 101 countries.

▶ TweetsGiving received over 100 press and blogger mentions.

Their success shows that even small organizations with limited name exposure can create communities to support nonprofits. Kaplan's blog (http://meshugavi.com/2008/12/the-story-beyond-the-stats-in-tweetsgiving) describes his thoughts on the metrics. Writing on her own blog (http://epicchangeblog.org/2008/12/05/why-tweetsgiving-worked-imho/), Monk describes elements of the campaign in detail, insights useful for other nonprofit appeals, and how ROI was worked out:

> To be honest, I wanted this experiment to be somewhat clean: I did not e-mail my regular list of donors to participate. A few caught it on our blog or on my Twitter-fed Facebook status, but this was very much engineered to appeal to potential donors who use Twitter. I had fewer than 10 Tweeters in my donor database prior to this campaign.

> I actually believe this campaign did far more to expand my network than to leverage my existing one. Only 6 out of 360 donors (< 2%) were previous donors to our cause, and I believe I've added about 500 new Twitter followers since TweetsGiving began. Over 98% of donors were people who had never before donated to Epic Change.

> Everyone can personally connect to the theme of gratitude. In addition, once people are feeling thankful, giving is a natural next step. It often takes substantial context to connect a potential donor with a small school in Tanzania thousands of miles away but, in this case, gratitude served as a universal connector to a common cause.

SPECIAL SECTION B

Marketing ROI Basics: A Refresher

We're well aware that many marketing professionals rise to heights in their organizations without formal training in finance. Or sometimes we get rusty when finance functions are handed over to a different department or one in a distant city. So, some basics are in order if you need a brief refresher on the mathematics involved.

Return on investment (ROI) isn't a magical formula for business success, but it is indeed a formula. It's a mathematical formula that is standardized for accounting. As mentioned, ROI can be used to measure success in terms of dollars, but its greatest unsung use in marketing is as a predictive tool—to make sure you are getting the most revenue return for each marketing initiative you launch.

We presented this classic formula for ROI earlier in Chapter 2, but it is worth repeating here for this refresher on ROI basics. Here's the formula again:

$$\text{(Net Revenues} - \text{Marketing Investment)} \div \text{Marketing Investment} \times 100 = \text{ROI \%}$$

You derive ROI by three steps:

1. Obtain a dollar figure that represents your *net revenues,* after subtracting a dollar figure that represents your spending, that is, your *marketing investment.*
2. Take that total (*net revenues* minus *marketing investment*) and divide it by the *marketing investment.*

3. Multiply this number by 100 to achieve the percentage result.

For those of you who never took *any* finance: yes, the *marketing investment* number is used twice in the calculation.

Example: if your revenues over the life of a campaign were $800,000, and the cost of the campaign was $100,000, the equation is:

$$(\$800,000 - \$100,000) \div \$100,000 = 7 \times 100 = \textbf{700\%}$$

Here's the equation again if you're really math-challenged: $800,000 minus $100,000 is $700,000; $700,000 divided by $100,000 is 7; 7 multiplied by 100 is 700. So, the ROI for this campaign is 700 percent, an astounding success.

Too bad it's not so easy to obtain success like this, let alone numbers so round and easily defined. In the real word, dollar figures themselves are hard to pin down, and that's where the real work of ROI-based marketing comes in.

Properly Identifying Your Variables Is Key

The key to good marketing ROI is making sure you've rounded up all the dollar figures involved in the first two parts of the equation, *net revenues* and *marketing investment*. This is trickier than it seems.

Net revenues may be the first number seen, and it is certainly the first number the C-suite and the accounting team will look at. However, for the marketing manager, the place to start is with the figures you are required to have at your disposal: the *marketing investment.* It certainly helps that this number is the one the marketing manager has most control over, and can change.

Determining the Marketing Investment Variable

To properly measure ROI, the marketing investment includes *only* those expenses that can be specifically attached to the campaign or an individual initiative.

For example, let's imagine a services company that has a new service to offer; the marketing manager plans a direct mail campaign to solicit orders for the new service, from old customers and new ones that might be interested as well.

The marketing investment might at first look something like this:

Creative (text and design for the mail piece), done in-house	0.00
List rental to augment existing mail list	$500.00
Printing and folding	$400.00
Postage costs	$1,000.00
Total investment:	**$1,900.00**

If the company used an outside agency to design the mailer and actually do the mail drop, the expenses would be more. Another issue is whether or not the in-house production of the mailer is really free. Should staff time, calculated by hours and salaries, be included in the number for marketing investment?

Best practices for ROI accounting suggest the answer is no. The only expenses to be calculated should be those specifically tied to the marketing initiative. If staff are paid whether they design mailers or do something else, their salaries are not subject to the ROI scrutiny. (The financial term for this is "sunk cost"—a prior expense that cannot be recovered.) But if the project required paid staff *overtime* for folding, stapling, and running a few thousand mailers through the Pitney Bowes postage meter, the expense of the overtime hours might thoughtfully be included here.

And, should the creative come from either an outside agency, a freelancer, or is charged back specifically to your department from the art department, it really must be included here to obtain an accurate ROI percentage result.

Anything that is an "up-front spend" for a marketing initiative is part of the marketing investment for that initiative. In the direct mail example, some paid market research done to identify words or colors best used in a mailer would also be an up-front spend, as it wouldn't have been paid for if the marketer hadn't been planning a mailer in the near future.

A helpful way to view your *marketing investment* is the way the finance department does. They view it as an expense made "at risk." This means that, if you weren't so stubborn that you wanted to spend money on a marketing project, they would be just as pleased if you never spend that money at all. They see your spending as money spent "at risk." As with other investments, the spending of money on marketing has to be seen as worth the risk.

Why would a company dare to risk any money on marketing at all? To increase *net revenue*, of course. The ROI number, which is always a percentage, is going to give them the odds, more or less, of whether your initiative will pay off in more *net revenue.*

Determining the Net Revenue Value

In order to weigh the risk of any marketing investment, a marketing manager needs to clearly understand not just that the initiative will bring in revenue, but—as accurately as possible—the amount of revenue that can be traced directly back to the initiative.

This is also harder than it looks on paper. On paper, *net revenue* is sometimes just *gross margin*, that is, the dollars from sales minus the dollars it took to create, sell, and distribute the product.

The latter is sometimes referred to in financial reporting for consumer products as COGS, or *cost of goods sold*. It's a simple calculation:

1. How much we took in this week, minus:
2. How much it cost to make, ship, and sell the product, which equals:
3. Our net revenue.

In the real world, it can be hard to calculate actual sales, let alone actual net revenues. And even harder to attribute them to a specific promotion, which is what you'd need to derive a true ROI.

One solution is to segment sales information into larger chunks of time, and/or for specific product campaigns that might have many different media initiatives but are united in theme or specific product. The usual time frame is monthly, although daily, weekly, and annual reporting is useful for other sorts of ROI reporting. Three-month reviews are also helpful, as they take into account the normal time frame for a sales funnel and revenue that may be thirty or sixty days behind billing or time of sale.

Another solution is to improve the tracking of a specific media initiative into the sales funnel. Online marketing provides extremely good tracking—so good that it's easy to get bogged down in tracking and forget the other elements that go into *net revenues*, such as cost of goods sold.

But traditional media can also be tracked. A magazine ad that includes a dedicated 800 telephone number is trackable; the phone system can count response rates variously. A customer calling center or sales rep at the other end of the phone can input into a CRM system the additional information useful for determining the overall success of the advertisement.

Other examples: a TV commercial that includes a website URL or text-message destination. An e-mail blast that contains a printable store coupon with a bar code is popular with firms that have a large brick-and-mortar presence, such as Barnes & Noble, which spits out three to five coupons per week during heavy shopping periods such as Christmas and June.

Online retailers use key codes for couponing; these are entered into a field during the checkout process and can thus be tracked to lots of useful customer data, such as order value per visit or tracking new customer response rates to that of existing customers.

Let's take a look at our services company again. The new service will be billed out at $50 per hour. This figure, minus the costs of producing the service, would be the net revenue.

Out of the $50 per hour, costs are as follows:

Cost of staff time .... $20 per hour
Cost of equipment needed to supply the service .. $ 2 per hour

We now know the product is designed to bring in $28 for each hour billed ($50 − $22 = $28). The product development team (for even service companies have product development teams) estimates that customers will on average request four hours of service per month.

So each customer is anticipated to bring in $112 of revenue for the first month following the mail launch. The marketing manager estimates the mail campaign will bring in forty new customers, and that at least sixty existing customers will also sign on for the additional service:

$$100 \times \$112 \text{ per month} = \$11,200$$

The projected net revenues are thus $11,200. So far. But the marketing manager wants to make this promotion trackable. On a mailer, one of the easiest things he can do is add a line like this: "For a 20% discount on your first month of service, mention Promo Code XYZ when you call our office."

That's a big gamble here for the marketing manager. New product discounts are common everywhere, but they come at a price. Removing 20 percent of the potential net revenue of the new service for its first month removes $10 from the sale of each service hour (now $40), while the expenses for each hour remain the same ($22). Each service hour is now worth only $18 to the company. If 100 customers sign up for the new service, and each customer still signs up for four hours, the projection is now:

$$\$18 \times 4 = \$72 \times 100 = \$7,200$$

Net revenues are now only estimated at $7,200. However, the marketing manager now has some basis for a projected ROI, using the formula:

$$(\$7,200 - \$1,900) \div \$1,900 = 2.78$$

Multiplying the figure by 100 gives the ROI percentage: 278 percent.

Projections Versus Reality

While the manager has a projected ROI, the actual ROI of the mailer won't be determined until the sales data arrives. Let's assume the news is not wonderful, but it's not too bad. Only twenty customers actually sign up for four hours of service; thirty-five customers try it at a two-hour level, and six customers try a single hour. All customers take the 20 percent discount.

Net revenues now look a little different for the first month:

20 customers @ 4 hours @ $18 per hour	$1,440.00
35 customers @ 2 hours @ $18 per hour	$1,260.00
6 customers @ 1 hour @ $18 per hour	$108.00
Total net revenues:	**$2,808.00**

The figures go into the formula:

$$(\$2{,}808 - \$1{,}900) \div \$1{,}900 = 0.47$$

Multiplying the final figure by 100 gives the ROI percentage: 47%.

That still looks pretty nice as a percentage, but the revenues that can be directly attributed to the mailer ($2,808) minus the cost of the mailer ($1,900) are only $908. A pittance, right?

If the product/service or the company has a bit of sales history, the *lifetime customer value* of each of the new customers can at least be estimated. Or in this case guesstimated, since the service offered is a new one.

A $908 profit only represents a first trip down the sales funnel for these new customers; it is up to the rest of the organization (sales support, fulfillment, customer service) to keep the customers returning for at least a few more rides.

When profits seem small at the onset of a campaign, it becomes more important to track results over the longer period of time.

This is even *more* important when the marketing department must shoulder part of the burden of overhead expenses.

If the marketing manager must include overhead costs of more than $908 into either the net revenue figure or the marketing investment figure, profits will disappear entirely and ROI be lower, be zero, or worse, become a negative percentage number.

Danger! Overhead!

Where does overhead go?

Whatever you do, don't allocate overhead costs to the marketing investment categories, unless your finance manager threatens to hang you upside down and beat you with a stick if you don't do it.

Plain and simply, overhead costs are not costs that can be attached to marketing investments. In financial accounting principles, marketing investments are—exclusively—the spending that you wouldn't spend if you were not undertaking a campaign.

In many organizations, overhead is allocated to the *net revenue* categories, usually by fiat of the CFO. This is not necessary and it skews ROI figures. It is inaccurate. The cost of creating and distributing a hard goods product, for example, includes the raw materials, shipping of raw materials and finished products, and worker salaries. It may also include, as a minus on the net revenue category, sales expenses (salaries, support services, discounts, and returns). But it does not include the rent on the factory. Or the CFO's leased Lexus. Or the potted plants that brighten up the office and the factory floor.

There's real danger in allocating overhead costs to individual campaigns and individual initiatives, on either side of the ROI equation. You run the risk of counting overhead costs more than once—the sales department may have already figured the organization's overhead costs as part of the cost of goods sold, and this amount has already been subtracted from the gross sales to derive the base net revenue for a specific product line. This is often true for hard goods and consumer products.

Smaller organizations, nonprofits, and service-based companies typically use a formula to distribute overhead costs among various departments. Rarely does the marketing manager have the opportunity to challenge the percentage allotment scheme (especially among nonprofits or academic institutions). Still, educating yourself, and the entire enterprise, to improve the allocation process is worthwhile if it can improve your numbers and hence your marketing ROI. (For strategies on this, see Chapter 5.)

If you are forced to add overhead expenses within your marketing budget, allocate carefully. When in doubt, make it a minus on the *net revenue* side. This may hurt your percentage numbers, but it will give you a better handle on the worst-case scenario financial results of your initiatives, relative to their costs, as the CFO sees it.

Comparing Marketing Initiatives Using ROI

Let's look back at our services company, and their mailing initiative. What would the numbers be like if they used e-mail, rather than the U.S. Postal Service?

The *marketing investment* might look like this:

Creative (text and design for the e-mail), done in-house   0.00
List rental to augment existing e-mail list $500.00
List management through e-mail fulfillment software,
including staff time to run program and cost of
    software $800.00

Total investment: **$1,300.00**

Again, handing any of the elements off to an outside e-mail marketing firm would increase the cost, but perhaps be offset by an increase in speed or skill level over what could be achieved using staff time alone. If e-mail management is done in-house, the cost of the software may (dangerously, as we've said) be an amortized expense to be allotted equally among all e-mail marketing initiatives planned over a one- to three-year period (or estimated life of the software).

If the e-mail software was bought specifically for this e-mailing, its entire cost may be considered an "up front" spend for this project. It would appear only in the marketing investment for this project, and no other, even if it is used again in the future. If the software cost is accounted to another department, such as IT, it does not belong in calculating the marketing investment for this project. If IT staff run the mailing program, the charge for list management could be $0 if their time is not charged back to the marketing department. However, the same concerns—speed of execution and skill level—would still need to be considered as tradeoffs. As they often are.

Let's get back to our marketing manager and his e-mail blast.

For the sake of argument, let's keep the projected revenues the same: $7,200 with the 20 percent offer of the first month of service.

And, also for the sake of argument, let's keep the results the same:

20 customers @ 4 hours @ $18 per hour $1,440.00
35 customers @ 2 hours @ $18 per hour $1,260.00
6 customers @ 1 hour @ $18 per hour $108.00

Total net revenues: **$2,808.00**

However, now the ROI equation is different:

$$(\$2,808 - \$1,300) \div \$1,300 = 1.16\,116 \times 100 = 116\%$$

Theoretically, the e-mail campaign has been more successful, but only because, in this example, the cost of the campaign was

$600 less. It's one good reason why many organizations have moved much of their direct-mail marketing into online marketing. It's also why organizations tend to rely too much on e-mail, and why today's marketing managers cling to it the same way their predecessors clung to high-priced TV ads or newspaper inserts.

We've used small numbers here to illustrate the basics. The numbers and the risks get bigger as the task does, and as they say on those high-priced TV ads, your own mileage may vary.

Hurdle Rates and Other Factors at Play

An ROI result is always expressed as a percentage. That percentage (zero being failure and any figure from there to 100% or more representing varying levels of success) is always a comparative figure. A ROI percentage of 116% sounds better than 47%, but both initiatives could be seen as successful.

In the real world, organizations usually have a specific percentage target in mind. This figure is often referred to as the *hurdle rate*. In general accounting, a hurdle rate may reflect the known return of other types of investments, such as a certificate of deposit that pays 3 percent over one year. Had the services company banked $1,300 instead of using it to pay for e-mail outreach, the profit during the same period—a month after the e-mail launch—would be one-twelfth of 3 percent, or $3.25. Apples to apples, financially speaking, and the e-mail initiative surely is the better deal.

In marketing, it's preferable to compare results and encouraging to do so. The hurdle rate of an e-mail campaign will be different from a print mail campaign. If management does not provide a hurdle rate, marketing executives should set their own goals for their department, and always aim high.

Decisions, Decisions

The marketing manager of our services company had a few choices to make. Not offering an introductory discount to improve tracking might have improved profits. But it might have inhibited sales, especially from the potential new customers on the rented list, or from existing customers reluctant to try the new service.

Other vehicles to launch the new service could also be used, such as a print media advertisement. More likely a barrage of initiatives would launch together, and the campaign as a whole could be measured over the first six months of sales for the new service.

The data itself can be a goldmine of help to sales, marketing, and the product development team. It may be determined, for example, that fifteen of the thirty-five customers who tried a two-hour trial were new customers entirely. A separate ROI equation could then be calculated to determine how successful the mailings—and the rented lists—were in obtaining new customers.

Marketing investment to obtain new customers would be calculated as follows:

List rental to augment existing mail list $500.00
Printing and folding* $200.00
Postage costs* $500.00

Total investment: **$1,200.00**

Costs are assumed to be half, if the rented list is half the total list.

Note that here the cost of in-house design is not included in the ROI calculation for new customer acquisition, as this would have been an expense anyway, to make the mailer for existing customers. Design costs are not specific to this part of the initiative.

Net revenues for new customers is calculated as follows:

15 new customers @ 2 hours @ $18 per hour = $540.00

ROI can thus be calculated as:

$$(\$540 - \$1200) \div \$1200 = -0.55 \times 100 = -55\%$$

Yes, it is possible to have negative ROI. In this example, the cost of the rented mailing list ($500) may appear to have "paid for itself" with the first month's revenues from the new customers. But we can't ignore the $700 for the additional printing, folding, and postage. This would not have been spent if the mailing had been sent only to the existing customer list. Unless the new customers can be tracked for lifetime value and continuing sales over time, the $1,200 to attract these new customers starts to look like a poor investment of the company's marketing dollars.

Yep, it cost the services company $80 apiece to acquire each of the fifteen new customers. One might argue that the fifteen didn't get a 20 percent discount on their services; in the eyes of the company, the fifteen new customers each got their first two hours of service entirely for free, because the marketing department paid for it. Ouch!

The takeaway: track, track, track results over time. Obtain the models for lifetime customer value (see Chapter 2) and compare results three months later. Your ROI results will probably be different (and we hope on the positive side!). CRM tools help, and marketers should always strive to obtain both sales data and data analysis to perfect their calculations for marketing ROI.

In our fictional exercise, information received is clearly actionable: the marketing manager can now decide if the cost of list rentals is worth the risk of losing money in the short term to attract new customers that will be profitable long term. That's why best practices for marketing ROI look beyond the marketing department, and into the silos of sales, public relations, customer support, finance, and IT.

Marketing ROI Glossary

A/B testing: Comparative testing that varies only one message element at a time.

acquisition cost: The total cost of acquiring a new customer.

buzz: A measure of "word-of-mouth" marketing and product reputation, representing excitement and conversation about a product or service.

click-through rate (CTR): The percentage of views on a web page that resulted in a desired click.

conversion: Generally, the purchase of a product or service by a web visitor. May also be used to define the completion of a desirable activity by a web visitor, such as site registration or newsletter subscription.

CPA (cost per action): The cost of generating a desired user click or purchase.

CPC (cost per click): How much is paid for the resulting number of user clicks on an ad or banner.

CPM (cost per thousand [mille]): A measure of the cost of paid advertising.

dashboard: An arrangement of gauges or measurements of real-time sales or marketing data that fits on a single computer screen.

DMA (designated market area): A specific geographic region served by radio and television stations.

exposure: A measure of the number of consumers who have seen or heard a media vehicle, whether or not they paid attention. Web page views, for example, are one rough measure of exposure.

frequency: The number of times a household will be exposed to a given media message or advertisement, whether or not anyone paid attention.

gross impressions: Total number of unduplicated people or households represented by a given media schedule.

GRPs (gross rating points): A measure of the advertising value delivered by an advertising vehicle within a specific time period. Determined by multiplying reach by average frequency.

impression: A single exposure to a marketing or advertising message.

influencers: Identifiable people (such as certain bloggers) who have a disproportionate influence on popular opinion about a product or service.

lead: An individual or organization that expresses an interest in a company's product or service.

lead generation ("lead gen"): The creation of consumer interest or inquiry into a business's products or services.

lifetime customer value: A calculation that allows you to quantify an estimate of all future purchases expected from a customer.

market share: The percentage of a product category's sales garnered by a brand or company.

open rate: A measure of how many people "view" or "open" an email message.

page views: The number of pages of a website viewed, often measured as the number of pages viewed by an individual viewer during one session.

peer-to-peer: Communication about a company's product or service from one individual to another, unmediated by the owner of that company, product, or service.

reach: The estimated number of individuals in the audience of a broadcast who view a message at least once during a specific period of time.

response rate: The percentage of people who responded to an offer.

retention rate: The rate at which customers or viewers return to a website or a store.

ROI (return on investment): The comparable percentage of profit generated by a specific marketing expenditure.

SKU (stock keeping unit): A unique identifier for individual products that helps keep track of inventories and sales.

share-thru: A measure of how many times a social media message (or video) is shared with friends or colleagues or referred to others.

time on site: How much time a user spends on a website.

trending: Being the most common topic or phrase appearing in a social media stream over a short period of time.

views: How many times a site or a video is viewed, usually during a specific time period such as a month.

unaided recall: The ability of viewers to recall information about an advertisement, product, service, or brand without being prompted.

uniques: The number of individual viewers for a website or a marketing message.

word of mouth ("word of web"): The spreading of information about a product or service from person to person.

Index